Inside Intermarriage

INSIDE INTERMARRIAGE

A Christian Partner's
Perspective on
Raising a Jewish Family

JIM KEEN

URJ Press · New York, New York

Versions of material in this volume previously appeared in
The Guide to Jewish Interfaith Family Life: An Interfaithfamily.com Handbook
and at http://www.interfaithfamily.com

For permission to reprint, please contact the URJ Press at:

URJ Press
633 Third Avenue
New York, NY 10017-6778

(212) 650-4124
press@urj.org

Library of Congress Cataloging-in-Publication Data

Keen, Jim, 1967–
    Inside intermarriage : a Christian partner's perspective on raising
a Jewish family / Jim Keen.
        p.   cm.
    Includes bibliographical references and index.
    1. Interfaith marriage.   2. Interfaith familiies.   3. Keen, Jim, 1967–   4. Keen, Bonnie,
1967–   5. Jewish families—Religious life.   6. Child rearing—Religious aspects—
Judaism.   I. Title.
    HQ1031.K39   2006
    306.84´3—dc22   2006045566

This book is printed on acid-free paper.

Copyright © 2006 by Jim Keen

Manufactured in the United States of America

10 9 8 7 6 5 4 3 2 1

To Bonnie, Gabrielle, and Molly,
whose love and laughter continually inspire me.

Acknowledgments

From the bottom of my heart, I would like to thank the following people: my parents and my wife's parents for their unending support, generosity, and love that made this book possible; my editor, Rabbi Hara Person, who so adeptly whipped this manuscript into shape; and all the great staff at the URJ Press, including Victor Ney, Ron Ghatan, Zack Kolstein, Lauren Dubin, Elizabeth Gutterman, Dahlia Schoenberg-Lain, and Debra Hirsch Corman.

I am also grateful to the contributors whose postscript pieces add their wealth of experience and knowledge: Dr. Paula Brody, Arlene Chernow, Rabbi Steven Einstein, Ruth Goldberger, Rabbi Howard Jaffe, Kathy Kahn, Karen Kushner, Rabbi Michelle Pearlman, and Julie Webb.

Special thanks to my readers, who made sure everything made sense: Jim Ball, Dr. Norman Cohen, Terry Cohen, Anita Diamant, Dru Greenwood, and Joyce Schwartz.

I would especially like to thank Ronnie Friedland, the editor of InterfaithFamily.com's Web Magazine. Ronnie expertly worked with me on the many articles I wrote for InterfaithFamily.com, where much of the material in this book originally appeared. Ronnie also pored through the manuscript of this book. She is a pleasure to work with, and I am very grateful to her. She and Edmund Case, publisher of InterfaithFamily.com, have created a much-needed resource for interfaith couples exploring Jewish life.

My gratitude also goes to the following people: Rabbi Bob Levy and the Reverend Bob Livingston, who welcome my family "as is"; Dr. Jay Sandweiss for his compass and good jokes; and finally, the many other friends and family members who encouraged me—or at least put up with me. So many words of appreciation come to mind, but just aren't worthy. Funny, I'm sure there's a Yiddish word for it.

Contents

Foreword by Rabbi Eric H. Yoffie

One of the great legacies of the Jewish Reform Outreach revolution, initiated by Rabbi Alexander M. Schindler, *z"l,* nearly three decades ago, has been to welcome non-Jewish spouses to our congregations. These spouses, who involve themselves in the activities of the synagogue, support the Jewish activities of husbands or wives, attend Jewish worship, and—most important of all—commit to raising Jewish children, are deserving not only of welcome but of our profound thanks.

These spouses are heroes—yes, heroes—of Jewish life. While maintaining some measure of attachment to their own traditions, and sometimes continuing to practice their religion, they take on responsibilities that, by any reasonable calculation, belong to the Jewish spouse. And very often they do all of this without recognition from either their Jewish family or their synagogue.

Jim Keen is one such hero. Although he continues to practice the Protestant religion in which he was raised, he and his wife Bonnie agreed before their marriage to raise their children as Jews, and today he is fulfilling that promise. In so doing, he has come to appreciate deeply the multifaceted richness of Judaism and strives—in a most selfless, deliberate, and introspective way—to transmit that heritage to his daughters, Gabby and Molly. Together with them and with Bonnie, as well as with his extended and synagogue families, he shares in the joys of meaningful Jewish living. Indeed, he is a success story for the Outreach revolution and for the Union for Reform Judaism, which spawned it.

Our obligation, in turn, is to extend our appreciation with a full embrace to Jim and to other remarkable individuals like him. To do so, we must ensure that our congregations and those who build the communities within them—from clergy and staff to lay leaders, and from ushers to educators—are *anshei chesed*, doers of goodness and purveyors of kindness who embrace the guest and welcome the traveler.

Without a doubt, Jim and Bonnie's congregation, Temple Beth Emeth in Ann Arbor, Michigan, is filled with *anshei chesed*. Led by Rabbi Robert D. Levy, Temple Beth Emeth exemplifies a sacred community of intimacy and warmth whose members feel safe, comfortable, and connected. It is a synagogue whose message of Torah is inspiring, whose spiritual energy is transforming, and whose web of kinship and caring embraces all who enter its gates. It is a place where, amidst all the frantic activity, members can sit down, have coffee and a bagel, and talk about what is happening in their lives, where they are supported in the deep—and day-to-day—experiences of life, where others notice when they are missing and take the trouble to find out why, and where a crisis is never faced alone. In short, Temple Beth Emeth is a model for us all.

So, too, is Jim a model for us all. We are deeply indebted to him and others like him who selflessly choose to instill the principles of our rich Judaic heritage and a deep love of Torah into their children, all without forsaking their own religious beliefs or practices. Their commitment to raise Jewish children means that these children, unlike others in interfaith families, are not being asked to choose between Mommy's religion and Daddy's religion and will not grow up lacking any sense of belonging within a religious community. Through their extraordinary and pioneering devotion, they are creating and enriching Jewish families, strengthening our destiny as a holy people, and remaining true to Rabbi Schindler's vision.

Rabbi Eric H. Yoffie
President, Union for Reform Judaism

Foreword by Kathy Kahn

Before 1970, only 13 percent of Jews were married to someone from a different religion. By 1979, the interfaith marriage rate for Jews had increased to 47 percent. As old prejudices faded, the American dream of tolerance, assimilation, and acceptance was coming true on a very personal scale. Opportunities increased for people of different economic, ethnic, and religious backgrounds to live and work together, establish relationships, and, in many cases, fall in love. In 1979, the Reform Movement of Judaism, under the leadership of Rabbi Alexander M. Schindler, *z"l*, recognized the need to address this demographic trend by establishing the Commission on Reform Jewish Outreach. One of the tasks of this commission was to encourage our congregational communities to welcome and integrate interfaith couples and to help them make Jewish choices for their families. For nearly three decades, thanks to the renewed commitment to Outreach by its current president, Rabbi Eric Yoffie, Reform Judaism has led the way in its commitment to applying the mitzvah of welcoming the stranger to all interfaith couples and their families.

These efforts have been blessed with success, and we have welcomed more interfaith families into our synagogues than all the other movements of Judaism combined. Nationally, nearly half the children in our Reform religious schools have one parent who was not born Jewish, but who is successfully, and with dedication, raising his or her children as Jews. Many times the partner who was not born Jewish has made the decision to convert to Judaism, but there are also many partners in interfaith relationships who do not. These partners, often active, valued members of our congregations, are committed to raising Jewish children with love, support, and pride even as they retain the religious identity of their birth. They have given us the priceless gift of their presence and, through their children, of another generation of Jews. The blessings that we have received by making Outreach to interfaith couples a priority of the Reform Movement are beyond counting.

Each interfaith couple has a unique story to tell about how they have faced the challenges and experienced the joys of being in an interfaith marriage. But we also know that there are common threads in each of these stories that run through many intermarriages. Some of these common issues arise within the relationship of the couple; other issues are tied to relationships involving family, community, religion, and tradition. Many other interfaith couples can learn from and relate to these individual stories, but few have been published. *Inside Intermarriage* is one of the first books authored by the Christian partner in an interfaith relationship that talks about raising a Jewish child with love, support, and integrity. It is a story told with humor and honesty about the intersection of two religious traditions in the life and loving relationship of one couple and their family. Their journey would not have been possible without the understanding and encouragement of clergy and congregation, which provided a path for them because of a deep commitment to Reform Jewish Outreach.

There are other voices who add their wisdom to each chapter of *Inside Intermarriage*. Experienced Jewish clergy and professionals, who have worked with and learned from interfaith couples and their families for many years, add their commentary in the postscripts that follow each chapter. Each postscript looks at the broader issues of interfaith relationships as they are introduced in Jim's story. Because of this commentary, *Inside Intermarriage* is a learning tool not only for interfaith individuals and couples, but also for their families and particularly for professionals and clergy who work with interfaith issues, such as communication between partners, relationships with extended family, parenting in an interfaith family, holiday celebrations, and honoring the tradition and religious identity of the partner who is not Jewish.

Like many interfaith couples, Jim and Bonnie have made a decision to raise their children as Jews. The unique part of their story is that they have decided to share their journey with all of us who read this book. The challenges they address and the joys that they experience echo those of many interfaith couples who, along with their families and communities, will learn much from the opportunity to see inside an intermarriage.

Kathy Kahn
Director of the Department of Outreach and
Synagogue Community, Union for Reform Judaism

Preface

Should I convert? Should I try to ask her to convert? If neither of us changes religions, can we get married? Who will officiate at the wedding? In what religion will we raise the kids? Wait, what will I tell my parents?

If you've picked up this book, chances are you've asked or heard these questions before. Being in an interfaith relationship can be scary. There's no point in denying it. It's purely frightening to be in love with someone so much, yet also to have this nagging feeling that your union will implode because of your religious differences. Don't lose hope, though. It is possible for the situation to be successfully resolved.

You needn't feel that you and your loved one are the only castaways in this lifeboat at sea. Today, many people are in interfaith relationships and going through the same gut-wrenching emotions that you are. In fact, according to the National Jewish Population Survey, one out of every two Jews who take the plunge is jumping into an interfaith marriage.

I am a Christian dad helping to raise a Jewish family. My wife, Bonnie, is Jewish. We have decided to raise our children Jewish. And while our family dynamics are in perpetual motion, we have made many of the tough decisions. I have written this book with the hope that others can learn from our experience.

It's no secret that interfaith marriages are complicated, especially when each partner is connected to his or her own religious faith and community. While I do not encourage interfaith marriages, I recognize that they have become a fact of our society. When this happens, this book can help those couples by sharing our solutions—ones that give the children a clear Jewish identity, yet where both partners can feel comfortable. Any family, no matter what the faiths of its individual members, can find our approach relevant. Interfaith homes come in all shapes and sizes. No two are alike. However, the foundations that will help them thrive are the same.

This book is not written solely for those readers who are interdating or intermarried. You may be a family member who is concerned for your son, daughter, sister, or brother who has entered into such a relationship. I have included material that is meant to be helpful to you as well. You may be asking questions like, "If my son marries outside our faith, will he be giving up who he is?" or, "If my sister's kids are raised Jewish, can I give them Christmas presents?" Perhaps you are a professional looking for a different perspective for the people you work with. Whatever your reason for reading this book, I hope you find it enlightening, entertaining, and helpful.

It all starts with dating—that is, if we can first overcome our basic differences. Then, before we know it, wedding plans emerge. And then, suddenly, the questions arise. What are we going to tell our parents? What kind of a ceremony are we going to have? Who is going to marry us? In what religion do we raise the children? How will we celebrate the holidays? Which ones? Yours or mine? Finally, how can each of us keep our own identity amongst all this give and take? It's not easy.

Read on. And, by all means, start talking with each other about the issues. There are workable solutions that will enable you to experience more joy in your marriage, your family, and your life. I promise that this book will help answer many of your questions.

Inside Intermarriage

Part I

INTERFAITH
DATING
Let the Issues Begin

1

When We First Discover Our
Religious and Cultural Differences

Do you remember when you saw your significant other for the first time? Your heart may have skipped a beat. You may have suddenly forgotten how to speak intelligibly. You may have even walked into a brick wall without noticing. Chances are, if you're Christian, you were only hoping that she'd agree to go out with you. Chances are, if you're Jewish, you were also hoping that she'd turn out to be Jewish too.

As an eighteen-year-old Protestant, making my way through my first year of college, I found out fairly quickly that interfaith dating wasn't going to be a piece of cake (as if any kind of dating is?). As a Christian, I had no idea what I was getting in to. My first clue came from just normal conversation. There were some very nice girls who liked to talk to me but whose conversation was sprinkled with Hebrew or Yiddish words that were unfamiliar to me.

Sometimes it felt like this: "Hi, my name is Jennifer, and last week at my sister's bat mitzvah, I sprained my ankle while dancing the hora, and that made me get *shmutz* all over my dress when I fell into a plate of chopped liver, which made my uncles mad, not because I made a mess, but because there actually was chopped liver, because the *simchah* was supposed to be *milchig*."

My response: "Hi, my name is Jim. What's *shmutz*?"

Of course, nobody in real life actually talks like this, except for the comedian Jackie Mason, but it just emphasizes how foreign the culture was to me. Even a few Yiddish and Hebrew terms, sprinkled here and there, made me realize that I had a lot to learn.

(By the way, if you're like I was, and don't understand a bunch of the Hebrew and Yiddish terms, look in the back of the book for definitions. I'll try to explain as much as I can as I go along, but, in the interest of fine literary flow, I may have to move on without an explanation.)

As a still-wet-behind-the-ears freshman, a conversation like that seemed to be a hint that the person was looking only for Jewish guys to date. However, looking back on it today, I can see that it was just a cultural difference that I did not yet understand. It was just like that first September when I was trying to figure out why a fourth of my dorm had gone home in the middle of the week. That's when my friend Jackie had to remind me that it was the Jewish High Holy Day of Rosh HaShanah. How would I know? It wasn't on *my* calendar.

Most of my Jewish dating edification came in college. Here I was, a freshman at the University of Michigan. The U of M gets a lot of its student body from all over the world. However, a good chunk of it comes from Massachusetts, New Jersey, and New York. In particular, many are from Long Island, New York. Many students from this area of the country are Jewish. Was I looking for Jewish women to date? No. But, my chances of meeting Jewish women were now proportionally higher than they were in high school.

While many of the Jewish women I met were giving me what I felt was a subtle signal of "I'm Jewish, so back off" (of course, there couldn't have been any other reason they didn't want to go out with me), I knew that there were some who would take the attitude, "What harm could it do if we take one day at a time?" By the second term of freshman year I met a woman named

Bonnie. Actually, I chucked a Nerf football at her as she walked by my dorm room door. She threw the ball back at me, I whipped it back at her, she ran down the hall with it, and our relationship had begun.

For the next week, before I got up the nerve to ask her out, we would bump into each other in the cafeteria. I didn't know that she was Jewish. I actually thought that she might be Italian. It didn't really matter to me. She was cute, so my brain went into caveman mode. "Me big strong he-man. You woman. Must have."

It worked. I didn't make too big of a fool out of myself. Bonnie liked me. We went out to see a mindless movie, and she still liked me. I don't even think she told me she was Jewish until our second or third date. She laughed when I told her that I thought she might be Italian. She informed me that the two cultures have a lot in common: family gatherings that revolve around food, talking with your hands, etc.

Of course, once we had unceremoniously informed each other what our religions were, it didn't take long to learn more specifics. Bonnie had grown up in the Conservative Movement of Judaism. She still felt that she belonged there. Some of her greatest memories were of getting together with her family for Passover and the High Holy Days. Being away at college for the first time ever, she also deeply looked forward to going back home to rekindle those feelings. She didn't keep kosher at the time, but her identity was strongly Jewish—religiously and culturally.

My story was very different. My grandpa Keen had grown up a Presbyterian in Oklahoma. As a young man, his prairie church once reprimanded him for attending a dance. So by the time he moved to Michigan in 1925, to become the university's head wrestling coach and to attend law school, he had found a different church to call home. That's how I was baptized a Methodist, instead of a Presbyterian. My family regularly went to services on Sundays, until we discovered hockey. My brother and I both played the sport.

Unfortunately, and much to the chagrin of my mother, hockey games were scheduled on Sunday mornings.

Notwithstanding our decreasing attendance at Sunday school, my parents made sure that my brother, sister, and I never lost our faith in God. We always said our prayers at night, and we tried to go to church as often as we could after the hockey season was over. By the time I became a freshman in college, I rarely went to services. Yet, even though I was out of touch with the church of my youth, I still believed in God. I still felt that Jesus was the Son of God. I still felt as Protestant as ever.

Despite being firmly rooted in our faith, my family had never stressed that there was only one true religion. As kids, we would ask my parents about Judaism or Islam. My dad always quoted my grandfather as saying, "Who's to say which religion is correct? There are many ways to explain God. All of them should be respected—except for those Lutherans." My grandpa Keen had a Mark Twain sense of humor.

Meeting Bonnie, I quickly discovered that many individuals from Jewish families have a strong desire to marry within their faith—more so than Christian families. A lot of this has to do with Jews being a minority. A lot of it has to do with the sheer tragedy of the Holocaust, still fresh in the minds of parents and grandparents. And much of it has to do with the fact that Judaism is both a culture and a belief system, whereas Christianity is primarily a belief system. You can be Jewish either religiously or culturally. You can be an atheist, but still strongly identify with Jewish culture and history. You can't be a Christian and not believe in God. You then become just American, or Scottish, or whatever your national heritage is.

It's not that Christians don't try to find other Christians to marry. Of course they do. Many Catholics may look for other Catholics to marry. Lutherans may look for other Lutherans. Greek Orthodox may seek other Greek Orthodox. What I didn't know, however, was that I was about to open Pandora's box. It never occurred to me that just dating could be a problem.

Whatever the backgrounds and circumstances, whatever the geographical origins, for some reason or another, Jews and Christians often find themselves falling in love. That's why you're reading this book. I hope I can straighten out some of this beautiful mess and show that the relationship does not have to end. People *can* work around their religious and cultural differences and live to tell about it. They may also find their lives exquisitely enhanced. How often do we get a chance to learn about, moreover, become a part of another culture? Many people view that as a chance to broaden their minds, build understanding, and breed tolerance. Intentionally or not, Bonnie and I were about to go down that path. But it would not be without struggle.

Postscript

We tend to think that the way we did things in our homes is the way to do them. This is true for any of us—Catholics, Lutherans, or Jews. Amanda's first Thanksgiving with Mark's family was difficult for her on many levels. Not only had she never been away from her parents on Thanksgiving, she also had never met Mark's Jewish family before this weekend. She was horrified to find that Mark's family did not serve mashed potatoes as part of their Thanksgiving meal. The mashed potatoes became the symbol of how very different she and her boyfriend were at the time.

The key is not to be afraid of the process of exploring both the similarities and the differences. In Amanda's case, she told Mark how much she missed her mother's potatoes, and he responded by telling her how much it meant to him that she was willing to spend this holiday with him. Not all issues will be as easy to resolve as the potatoes, but couples who often have problems tend to be those who are afraid to begin the process of the exploration and discussion.

Couples who are attracted to each other and then become aware of interfaith differences need to be able to create or find safe places to explore many questions. What role did religious identity play in my home when I was growing up? What religious identity and community do I want for my children? What role do I want religion to play in my future? What is my relationship to God? How much of what I cherish is cultural, and how much of it is religious? Having the courage to be open and clear about these issues should make you realize that the fear of the discussion was much worse than the discussion itself.

A. C.

2

The Relationship Turns Serious: Now What?

I'm from Ann Arbor—the home of the university. Had I socialized with Jewish girls before? Sure. I had even dated a couple in high school. Ann Arbor has a very diverse population. However, I was totally clueless as to the cultural differences between Christians and Jews. The reason? Probably because in high school, the dating wasn't as serious. I wasn't looking for the love of my life there. While many people at that age do find the one they will eventually marry, I wasn't expecting to do so. Therefore, if the phrase "marrying outside the faith" came up with my high school girlfriends, I don't remember. I wasn't really paying attention. After all, we were only going to the movies.

In college, however, many relationships turn more serious. People consciously or unconsciously look for partners who will fit their notion (and their parents' notion) of the ideal spouse. Even though I didn't exactly fit the bill, being Protestant and all, it looked like my relationship with Bonnie had potential. In the back of my mind, I knew that she was Jewish and we might have problems. But, at the moment, it didn't matter that we were of different religious and cultural backgrounds. We were having fun together and taking one day at a time.

As the semester continued, our relationship blossomed. Her grades went up, mine went down, and suddenly, we had summer break staring us in the face. Panicking, I asked, "What do we do? I'm from Ann Arbor; you're from Boston." It dawned on us that we were going to have to be apart for a few months. Nonetheless, we were still a couple and would not break up. The last few months had been wonderful. As different as our backgrounds were, we had so much in common and found it very easy to be together. Yes, we were getting serious.

Mike, my housemate, once asked me, "When did you know you were serious with Bonnie?" He had been dating someone for a couple months and was starting to get that feeling.

"Do you remember your previous girlfriends," I asked, "how, when you would have an argument, that was the end of the dating? Well, you know you're serious when you have a fight about something, and all of a sudden, it matters to you. It hits you like a ton of bricks, 'I want to work this one out. I don't want to break up.' That's when you know you're serious."

So, Bonnie and I made plans to visit each other twice during the summer. In June, she would come to see me in Ann Arbor. In July, I would go to see her in Boston.

Bonnie's trip to see me at my parents' home was uneventful— great fun, but nothing unusual happened. After all, she had gotten to know my mom, dad, brother, sister, grandparents, and dog during the school year. They lived in the same town.

My parents had had a couple of small conversations with me about the difficulties that lay ahead by getting more serious with Bonnie. They never told me that they disapproved, though. They simply let me know that when people of two different religions get married, conflicts often arise, and solutions are hard to come by. Despite their concerns regarding my bold steps into this relationship, they already loved Bonnie. She was smart, she was funny, and she could dish it right back to my sarcastic brother, Tom. What was not to like?

My visit to Boston, to see Bonnie and meet her family, was a little different. It was great fun, once again, but quite eventful. She had warned me that meeting her dad might be a little different. "Why?" I asked.

"Because you're not Jewish."

"So?"

"*So,* when you're a Jewish girl, you grow up thinking that you're going to, someday, marry a 'nice Jewish boy.' My dad likes to perpetuate that idea. He's a Conservative Jew and was raised Orthodox. He has very traditional feelings about things like this."

This issue had come up over the last few months, but we had continued to brush it aside. They were the kind of conversations that we mentioned casually while lying around the dorm room studying—half concentrating on each other, half focusing on a political science midterm. We weren't *that* serious, were we? We weren't talking marriage—yet. So, the reality never hit home. Or, at least, we had not let it.

Even though we were not even close to being engaged yet, Bonnie and I now knew that our relationship was becoming more and more meaningful every day. She had always thought that she'd marry within her religion, but now she wasn't so certain.

As it happened, she introduced me to her father, stepmother, mother, and stepfather. Yes, I had not one, but two encounters of "meet the parents." I never had to hook up to a lie detector test, but because Bonnie's parents were divorced and remarried, I did have to go through that initial meeting twice. For all of Bonnie's parents, except her father, my being Christian didn't seem to be much of an issue. Or if it was, they never let it be known. They made me feel very welcome.

I knew that her dad would have been a lot more comfortable had I been Jewish. Nonetheless, we had a nice visit. He began to relax when he found out that my favorite movie was *Mary Poppins*—his favorite, as well. It turns out that we enjoyed a lot of the same films. This gave us something in common that we could focus our attentions on. My breathing began to return to normal, too. All of us knew that we had a few more years of college before any talk of marriage would arise. Who knew what could happen in that time, so why force the issue now?

That was the first summer. But then came the second summer. We were still in love and still determined not to break up. Then came the third summer, and I think our parents (all three sets of them) started to figure out that we were serious. This relationship quite possibly was going to lead to marriage. During this time, I saw her family in Boston, and sometimes they would come out to Ann Arbor for a campus visit. In addition, my parents saw us frequently at Michigan football, basketball, and hockey games. We all got along amicably, despite not having figured out the issue of religion.

Bonnie's father and I did have a couple frank discussions where he told me his feelings of unease at the idea of a Protestant man marrying his daughter. He explained to me how the Jewish tradition was very important in his family. Intermarriage just wasn't done. He was concerned that Bonnie would lose her Jewish identity. He was also afraid that any children we had would not be Jewish. One of the issues of particular importance to him was that he felt that after the Holocaust, Jews needed to preserve their numbers. If intermarriage became commonplace, the culture and religion would be in danger of dying off.

Although he said that he would love it if I converted, he never pressured me and always made it clear that he liked me regardless of religion. The talks that he had with me were more about whether we had found a solution, rather than telling me what to do.

Because we had been able to communicate openly, Bonnie and I understood what made her dad uncomfortable and why. She shared a lot of his feelings and, moreover, did not want to disappoint him. Although she had heard stories of children being disowned when they intermarried, Bonnie didn't think it would get to that point in hers. Yet, she wanted his approval very much. We were also in love, and she did not want to give up on that. I knew that the conflicting feelings ate at her. Though I had not yet figured out how we would resolve our differences, my biggest fear was less about tradition, children, and conversion, and more about whether Bonnie would decide that getting married was simply too complicated. I wanted—and needed—her dad's approval very much, too.

Bonnie and I began to talk more earnestly about possible solutions. Would I convert? I really did not want to. I knew the idea of her converting was not even worth bringing up. Could we just manage to maintain our respective religions in peaceful coexistence? Could we raise our children in both religions? Or, should we pick one of the religions and raise them solely in that? I understood Bonnie's feelings about not wanting to give up her Jewish faith and identity. I did not want to give up my Protestant faith and identity, either. I wasn't sure how I'd feel about my children not believing that Jesus was the Son of God. Despite all this, we were both very committed to somehow making it work. But this sure was becoming a lot of mental anguish for something that started out as a simple date to see a Pee-wee Herman movie.

By the fourth summer, we had graduated from college. Who knows what possesses a man to propose marriage, but I did it that Memorial Day. I admit that it was somewhat impulsive. I had an overwhelming feeling of love for this woman, and I didn't want to let her get away. We were out of school and heading toward our next stages in life. I was going into my family's business, and Bonnie was headed to law school. We had been dating for over three years, and the time was right to make the commitment.

Perhaps somewhere in the back of my mind was the idea that engagement would force us to reconcile our issues a little faster, too, instead of just waiting for some solution to pop into our heads. However, we decided not to set a wedding date right away. We both felt strongly that we couldn't say our nuptials until we had arrived at a resolution. We were now officially serious—diamond ring serious. Yet, we still had no clue as to how we would resolve our religious differences.

Postscript

Most of us grow up with the assumption that we will someday wind up with someone who is culturally, religiously, or racially similar to us. But in college or while traveling or at work, you might meet someone charming, someone insightful, someone whose values and interests seem to match yours perfectly, even though their background is different. In the glow of growing affection, whatever differences there are between you seem to recede in comparison with all that you share.

The first visit home to introduce this special person to your parents can cast the first shadow on that loving glow if you don't prepare yourselves and your parents. Your parents love you and want you to be happy. Suddenly, however, they may need to adjust long-held assumptions about your future. The idea that these assumptions might not actually happen can create a sense of loss or even panic and despair for parents of any religion or background.

Your parents, sad that a certain picture of the future they had hoped for might be lost, may worry that you do not see potential complications of continuing your relationship. You may worry that your parents don't see how wonderful your partner is and how much you get from the relationship. Each set of parents has to cope with a future they may not have been expecting. It will be up to you to clarify for yourselves what religious values and expressions you want to hold on to as you continue to build a relationship with each other and with your extended families. Meeting each other's parents helps to jump-start that conversation. It is essential that you all move beyond the worrying and get to know each other.

Tips to help make the visit go smoothly:

1. Ask your parents to wait until they have met your partner before making assumptions about your future.

2. Whenever you can, reassure them about your love and commitment to your family.

3. *Find points of commonality for your parents and your partner. Emphasize both common interests and common values. Make sure your parents know all that you love and appreciate about this person. Make sure your partner knows all that you love and appreciate about your family.*

4. *Plan activities together. It is easier to get to know someone in the course of an activity, whether it is hiking or gardening, playing volleyball or baking cookies.*

5. *Put yourself in the shoes of both sets of parents. Anticipate what problems they will worry about and think about them carefully so that you are prepared to talk about their issues with them.*

K. K.

3

When Did I Become
a "Non-Jew"?

As my conversations with Bonnie kept ending with talk of still more talk, our engagement continued. Bonnie and I kept visiting with each other's families. We went to hockey games together, we went to dinner together, and we went to holiday gatherings in each other's family homes. She learned a lot about my family; I learned a lot about her family and Judaism. It seemed like there was never a moment when someone wouldn't take the opportunity to explain one aspect or another of the Jewish religion or culture to me.

"Every Friday night is Shabbat, or the Sabbath," my future father-in-law would tell me. "This is when we have a 'Friday night dinner.' *Shabbes* is the most important of all Jewish holidays."

"Oh?" I would answer innocently. "When is *Shabbes*?"

"Every Friday night."

"I thought Shabbat was on Friday."

"It is."

"What's the difference between Shabbat and *Shabbes*?"

Seeing my confusion, he answered, "Nothing. They're the same thing. *Shabbat* is the Hebrew word for the Sabbath; *Shabbes* is the Yiddish."

"What's the difference between Hebrew and Yiddish?"

"*Oy.*"

My education was just beginning. One summer evening, Bonnie's dad and I were talking amicably about Jewish holidays. Taking a twisted ram's horn down from the shelf of his Boston living room, he asked me if I knew the name of this common Jewish symbol. For some reason, I remembered the word "chauffer" from watching it blown during a Rosh Hashanah service that I attended with Bonnie. "Shofar," he corrected me. Then he asked me if I could blow it. All I can say is, thank goodness I used to play trumpet in my junior high band. I think I grew three inches right in front of him at that moment.

Bonnie's other parents also liked to teach me about Judaism and its culture. Her stepfather and I discussed Israeli politics together (something that I never had an interest in before). He also enjoyed teaching me expressions in Yiddish (in which he is fluent). Her mother and grandparents fed me (copious amounts) of various Jewish foods. I learned what a kugel was and the proper way to pronounce it. And, Bonnie's stepmother taught me a lot about women in Jewish history—something I am grateful to pass on to my daughters today.

This learning experience was all very nice. However, while everyone was trying to accommodate me, I couldn't help but feel a little conspicuous. I knew that Bonnie's family went through the pains of teaching me because they were trying to *include* me. In their efforts to help me fit in, though, I was starting to feel even more like an outsider.

Suddenly, I was a "non-Jew." It's a crazy feeling discovering you're a "non-something." You usually walk through life thinking of yourself as a "something," but never the opposite of something. I can safely say that, on my census form, I've never put down "non-female" or "non-dependent" or "non-sixty-five-year-old."

This feeling began to grow during the Passover seders, Thanksgivings, and other get-togethers with her parents and extended family. The first time we gathered together with her aunt, uncle, and cousins was a big Thanksgiving weekend on Long Island. Her cousin James had just gotten married. His wife Janice was also from the area, and her parents came to the dinner, too.

This was also the first chance the family had to view the wedding video together. Here it was, my first night with everyone (the whole *mishpachah*), and we sat down in front of the VCR and TV. The wedding looked like a lot of fun. I saw James break a glass, I saw people dancing in a circle, and I saw lots of food.

I also got to hear Uncle Sidney's toast. Part of it went, "Roses are red, violets are blueish. We all love Janice, and thank God she's Jewish." Everyone in the video laughed uproariously. Those sitting in the living room started to chuckle, then stopped as they remembered that I was there.

Cousin Ken leaned over to me as the video played on and asked if it had made me feel uncomfortable. "Uncomfortable? Heck no," I replied. "That was hilarious." And it was. I can recognize good humor when I see it. It takes a lot more than that to offend me. I still felt different from everyone else. It takes a few years for that feeling to dissipate. I didn't feel annoyed or hurt—just different and maybe a little lost.

At the same time that I was experiencing how it felt to be different and an outsider, spending time with Bonnie's family was also making me want to become a part of her family—from her parents down to her aunts, uncles, and cousins. Despite the differences, I liked them. I wanted to fit in.

Later that night, as we all went to bed in her uncle's house, the lights had no sooner turned off when somebody accidentally (and loudly) banged into a big brass ship's bell in the kitchen. "Time to get up!" roared Uncle Sid. I could hear everyone laughing from inside his or her room. A bell also went off in my head. Her family was not so different from mine. We enjoyed good conversation and funny jokes, and we had a lot of the same personalities. Looking back on that weekend, it was actually the beginning of my journey of belonging, of losing the feeling of being a non-Jew. I began to see that though I wasn't Jewish, I could still fit into the family as myself. Despite our differences, we had things in common.

It wasn't just that one weekend that made me feel like I didn't stick out. But as silly as it was, that incident was the start. I now had the desire to discover more about Judaism. Over time, and through many Jewish events, I took the opportunity to learn. I also became more comfortable in my new Jewish surroundings. Each year, the feeling of standing out lessened.

That's the thing about Bonnie's family. They went out of their way, right from the start, to make me feel a part of the group. Whenever something Jewish came up, like a ritual or an expression, they took time to explain it to me. They translated Hebrew blessings into English for me. On Passover, they told me the significance of each object on the seder plate. It took a few years, but I really did begin to feel comfortable with saying the blessings, with performing the different holiday rituals, and with knowing that her family was welcoming me in. As time went on, they began to think of me as part of the landscape. I was a reality, and they accepted me. Knowing this only made me want to participate more.

I think I felt like a "non-Jew" because I was learning a whole new culture all at once. It's like being the new kid in school, or showing up late for a meeting and having everyone fill you in on the project. It takes a while for you to feel truly involved.

There were other issues bothering me at the time, too. I couldn't help but wonder, by learning and participating in so much Jewish ritual and culture, if I was starting to lose my Christian identity. Was Jesus OK with this? It may sound funny, but how was I to know? I knew that I was still Christian. I still had my faith. But sometimes, when I was feeling particularly guilty that I might be abandoning my upbringing, I made sure to get to church that Sunday. One time, Bonnie asked me why I always wanted to head to church right after the High Holy Days. It was at that moment that I realized what I needed to do—relax. I was a Protestant all year round. I didn't have to get a dosage of Christianity every time something Jewish happened. I could still learn about Bonnie's faith and culture without undermining my own. How else were we to come together as boyfriend and girlfriend? As husband and wife?

During the period when Bonnie and I were dating, she taught me several terms for non-Jews. I'm told that some of these may be offensive in certain contexts, so be careful how and when you use them.

Gentile is a word that most non-Jews have heard. It basically refers to anyone who isn't Jewish.

The Yiddish word for gentile is *goy*. You may hear this word when Cousin Rachel brings her non-Jewish boyfriend, Chris, to a wedding. Aunt Silvie will say, "Oy, he's a *goy*." The plural of this word is *goyim*, which means "nations" in Hebrew. It comes from the sense of "people of other nations." As a boy, Colin Powell, a four-star general and the former secretary of state, was a *Shabbes goy*. That is a non-Jew who is hired by Jews to do various tasks around the synagogue or a Jewish home on Shabbat (the Jewish Sabbath)—jobs like lighting the fire that are technically considered work, and therefore forbidden on that day. Legend has it that Powell learned to speak fluent Yiddish by doing this, a skill that impressed his Israeli counterpart at their first meeting many years ago.

Moving toward the less refined of terms, *shiksa* refers to a non-Jewish woman. It is often used to refer to the archetypical blonde, non-Jewish woman. Today, its use is more general. It is important to note, however, that though this word is used casually in everyday conversation, its origins are quite unpleasant. It actually comes from the Hebrew word used in the Bible to mean "abomination."

One last expression that I'd like to cover is member of the Tribe. No, I'm not talking about the Cleveland Indians. The Tribe, in this case, is the Jewish people. My friend Matt invited me to a fundraiser for the Holocaust Memorial in Detroit. During dinner, one of his

Jewish friends said to me, "You're not a member of the Tribe, are you?" The comment was not one designed to exclude or ostracize me. In fact, it was said during the friendly conversation we were having about Michigan football. How it fit into that exchange, I'll never remember. Sometimes this term is shortened to M.O.T.

I can see where use of these words and phrases can make a non-Jew (now even I'm using the term) feel out of place, particularly around a group of strangers with whom you're trying to fit in. As I found out, even some Jews are not comfortable with their usage.

I do want to point out that feelings of not belonging are natural and expected. On Shabbat, I was constantly afraid of drinking the wine at the wrong moment during the *Kiddush*, the blessing over the wine. I was nervous that I would break off too big of a piece of challah during the *Motzi*, the blessing over the bread. On a couple of occasions, I nearly blew out the Shabbat candles instead of letting them burn completely down. Of course, my mind ran away with what the punishment might be for such an offense. I imagined the family having to read the entire Torah in one breath, while fasting for forty days.

You should have seen me the first time I went to temple with Bonnie and her parents. I was sure I was going to get "outed" right there in the synagogue, in the middle of the service. I thought the rabbi would look up and see me, the only one not reciting the prayer in Hebrew, and have me tossed out. I later found out that many Jews don't know the Hebrew, either. Turns out I *could* blend in after all.

Yet, I persevered. What made me want to keep learning—keep putting myself in situations of anxiety and potential ostracism? This was not the familiar, comfortable territory that I had grown up with. I guess it had to be love. There are simply some things worth getting sweaty palms over.

Before I make it sound too easy, not every member of every family will go out of his or her way to make you feel welcome. I consider my experience fortunate. However, there are family members for whom it takes a while to get comfortable with the idea that someone in the family is inter-dating or intermarrying. This may come in the form of avoidance, not being included in family functions, not attending one of your functions, or even outright, in-your-face confrontation. Just try to understand the source of their dissatisfaction before you pass judgment back on them. Some people may simply be close-minded. Some may be open-minded, but unable to accept your relationship based on their religious beliefs. Some may not even care about your non-Jewishness. They just may not like you because you wouldn't eat their gefilte fish.

Whatever your experience, don't let the ups and downs take a toll on your relationship with your partner. Bonnie and I had a few heated discussions about unrelated matters, but often found them to be incited by feelings of not fitting into the other's religious activities. Sometimes I didn't want to let myself enjoy the experience, scared that I might lose my own identity. Other times, Bonnie was not comfortable with being a part of my Protestant culture or participating in my religious celebrations. One Christmas Eve, we were planning on attending the church service with my family. Bonnie and I had already established our game plan that she was only going to help me celebrate my holiday. But, all throughout the day, we found ourselves squabbling about everything in sight—the right thing to wear, the possibility that my mom might use Christmas wrapping paper on a gift for Bonnie, the dishes not washed. You name it, it became a point of contention that day. And, this was *after* we had been married for a couple years.

When we finally analyzed it, we were both a little nervous about the holiday and how we would *both* fit in. There would be Bonnie—a Jewish woman in a Protestant church. What should Bonnie do while there? There would be me—the Protestant guy with the Jewish wife. How do I act at church now? How do I participate without looking like I'm trying to make up for having gone to temple? How do I make Bonnie comfortable? Growing up as a minority and being overwhelmed by the Christmas marketing season, Bonnie had never felt that great about this holiday. In fact, it made her uneasy at times.

Once we were able to get to the heart of the issue and realize the root of our anxiety, we knew that things would be better. We both were trying to fit in. At least we would give the bickering a rest for a while. We were in this together and that was comforting.

It took a little time, but learning more about each other's religion was actually a lot of fun. We began to feel a sense of purpose and determination to research as much about our religions as possible. The more we were informed, the better our decisions would be. In addition to learning from each other and our families, we attended an introduction to Judaism class together and talked to an intermarriage counselor.

It also helped me to feel comfortable with being a non-Jew in her presence, in her family's presence, and while participating in Jewish activities. With my ever-growing knowledge of Judaism, I was able to know what to expect ahead of time.

Being a non-Jew involved with a Jew can bring about an overwhelming set of feelings. As I got more comfortable with the Jewishness of Bonnie and her family and friends, I found myself being able to move in and out of that group, depending on the situation. Now, on the Jewish holiday of Sukkot, I can feel that I'm part of the celebration. One day, I can build the sukkah, shake the *lulav* and *etrog*. The next day, I can turn around and go to church, feeling just as Protestant as ever. In the early days of our relationship, I couldn't do that. I would not allow myself to enjoy a Shabbat dinner or synagogue service, because I was too afraid that I was doing a disservice to or losing sight of my own religion. However, as I continued to attend church and celebrate the Christian holidays with my family, I learned that I could do both. I could still be a Christian *and* help Bonnie enjoy her religion and family get-togethers. I had to try it to know that my Protestant faith wasn't going to disappear simply because I helped someone else experience her religion. I would still be able to spend the holidays with my family, and I would still be able to love Jesus. It may sound strange, but I would still be able to watch

"A Charlie Brown Christmas" on TV. Time and experience showed me that Snoopy wasn't going anywhere.

Postscript

Bethany and Benjamin had been dating for two years, starting when they were both in the Peace Corps in Uganda learning a language and a foreign culture. With all her skills in biculturalism, Bethany was expecting an easy time fitting in with Ben's family for the week of Passover. Ben told her that his family was not very observant of the laws of the holiday, and he was looking forward to showing off the bright, caring woman he loved very much. His family had spoken to Bethany on the phone and was excited and eager to meet her.

It was thus a huge shock to find his normally very secular family insisting on reading every page of the Haggadah. Not only that, but his very fashionable, worldly grandparents were using Yiddish expressions and telling "injokes" that made Benjamin lose his appetite. Bethany had never before felt like a non-anything, but suddenly she was very aware of her non-Jewish status.

Bethany worked hard to follow the confusing progression of the Passover ritual and found it as difficult as her early days in Africa. Ben helped as much as he could but found he could not answer most of Bethany's questions. Later that evening, Benjamin realized that his family had reacted to Bethany's Christianity by overemphasizing their Jewishness. Bethany alternated between being angry and sad over what felt like a rejection by Benjamin's family and an indication of what might be a lifelong struggle with her future in-laws.

Through honest conversations over a period of time and a growing sense of mutual trust, these feelings were eventually dispelled. Though Benjamin's parents and Bethany grew to value, love, and respect one another, it was an awkward and confusing beginning that took patience and understanding on everyone's part to overcome.

K. K.

4

Before We Go Any Further, What Religion Would Our Children Be?

Bonnie and I had started to discuss the issues about our different religious backgrounds over that period of time leading up to our engagement. Bonnie's dad was still uncomfortable with the idea that I wasn't Jewish. On top of it all, her Orthodox grandmother, or *Bubba* as she called her, told Bonnie that she wished her well, but couldn't go to our wedding. It was a matter of principle for her. It's things like these that get you talking about the details in a hurry.

Having members of her family not one hundred percent behind her put a great strain on Bonnie. Sometimes she felt as though she were being forced to make a choice between her family and me. Of course, this put me under a lot of stress, too. Not only did I hate to see my fiancée go through this anguish, but also I worried that it would spell the end of our relationship. This was not going to happen. We both understood that we would have to find a solution.

How would we resolve our differences? We knew that we wanted to spend the rest of our lives together. But how could we if we couldn't figure out the religion question? I was comfortable with her being Jewish. She was fine with me being Protestant. We had explored the idea of one of us converting.

It wasn't simply a matter of, "You convert."

"No, you convert."

I don't think either one of us felt right about asking the other to make such a profound change. We knew each other too well. We knew that our identities were important to us. And, although I was learning about Judaism, I still didn't know it well enough to say, "Hey, I like this a whole lot better than Christianity."

So, the conversations were more about, "What if one of us were to take classes about the other's religion, then that person could decide . . . no that won't work. Forget I said it."

In the end, we decided that it was too much to ask of one of us. We were both fairly religious and rooted in our faiths. I had seen other couples where one partner converted. In some cases, it seemed that the one who made the switch had already been searching for a spiritual home, or hadn't been deeply connected to another faith. For whatever reason they chose that route, for those couples, it was probably a good decision. But, we knew that we would never feel comfortable during our marriage if one of us left the faith and background that had meant so much to us.

Bonnie and I had to think about the real motivations behind conversion. A counselor we talked to and the books we read reinforced our decision. When someone converts, it should be for the right reasons. You should feel that the change helps you become more of your true self. Our religious identities were tightly woven into the fabric of our families, to whom we were very close. Making a change in our religious identities would have to be an authentic choice for either of us.

We did not want to make such a drastic life change just to please each other or our parents. That would be the wrong reason to do so and would probably lead to years of unresolved resentment. I knew that Bonnie's dad would be disappointed. But at the same time, I felt relief that Bonnie backed me up with her father. Conversion to

Judaism simply wasn't going to happen. We would make it work another way.

That part was settled. Bonnie would continue to be Jewish, I would still be Protestant. We felt that we had reached an important milestone, but we were still nowhere close to solving the problem. Our discussion then started to center not on what religion we would have, but on what religion our kids would have. Children? (See Jim. See Jim's head spin.) We promised each other that somehow we would have it ironed out before the wedding. This was a toughie.

We certainly had our work cut out for us. Fortunately, we weren't alone. Our parents, even her dad, cared more that his daughter was marrying someone she loved, and someone who loved her, than that she marry a fellow Jew. Our parents came to realize that we made each other happy. They offered us not so much advice, but support. Meanwhile, Bonnie and I continued to talk and talk and talk and talk.

It seems like just yesterday we were freshmen and meeting for the first time in the dorm at the University of Michigan. Although it only took a couple of dates before we brought up the subject of our different religions, neither one of us cared too much to dwell on it. We weren't serious yet. We were just going out.

"Wanna go see *The Rocky Horror Picture Show* Saturday?"

"OK. Pick you up at eleven."

At that point we were more concerned about exams than we were about who celebrated Christmas and who celebrated Chanukah. Kids were definitely the last thing on our minds. I think we both knew that we would get married someday, but now the issue of our differing religions began to play an ever-important role. Simply being married to a person of a different faith was a tough issue, but certainly workable. Aside from the wedding day itself, the thought of just the two of us going through life wouldn't be so difficult. You celebrate your holidays; I'll celebrate mine. It could be a sort of "live and let live" attitude. However, this was not the kind of relationship we had envisioned having forever. We both, eventually, wanted children. There was the problem.

"I'm comfortable with you being Christian, but I would like the kids to be Jewish," Bonnie had said.

"I'm alright with you being Jewish, but I'm not sure how I'd feel if our children did not believe in Jesus as the Son of God," I replied. I had always been tolerant and respectful of other religions. Suddenly, though, I wasn't so sure how I'd feel if my own children had a different set of beliefs.

Impasse reached.

This is where most interfaith couples realize the complexity of their situation. It's one thing to be tolerant and accepting of another person's religion, but it's a whole other world when you bring your children into the picture. These will be my offspring—my legacy—the ones who will carry our family name and traditions into the future. The possibility of raising your children in a religion that is not your own can be an overwhelming thought to fathom. I also had to picture my role in raising my children in a different faith. Would I feel a part of the family? Would I know what to do?

Fortunately, even though we were in love, we didn't just jump into marriage without first working this issue out. We got engaged knowing that we couldn't get married until we had found a solution. During the next two years, we talked about the dilemma constantly. We also read what few books there were on interfaith marriage. Unfortunately, there was no InterfaithFamily.com or books from any different points of view yet. We could have used such resources.

We weren't without assets, though. Bonnie's stepmom just happened to be a social worker who specialized in interfaith relationships. In this role, she helped us navigate through many of the tough interfaith issues. We also sought the wisdom of our other parents. While not experts in the field, they gave us sound advice based on common sense and life experience.

All of the input certainly helped. However, I would say that what worked best for us was just the hours and hours of talking to each other and trying to figure out what our religion meant to each of us.

Every once in a while, our conversations would get heated, but we never for a minute wanted to give up. We knew we had come too far and loved each other too much to let anything get in the way of our spending the rest of our lives together.

In many interfaith families, the partner who is less religious often offers to raise the children in the other spouse's faith. Our problem was that we were both pretty religious, had strong family ties, and had wonderful memories of celebrating the holidays with our respective families.

In the end, we decided to raise the kids Jewish—partly because Bonnie would be moving away from her family in Boston to live with me in Ann Arbor, where I was born and raised. She felt that a lot of her Jewish identity was a direct result of being around her parents and cousins. Raising our kids Jewish would help her feel that she was still in a Jewish home. On the other hand, I would still be living in the same town as my Christian family. In addition, because Bonnie had come from a Conservative Jewish background, she had grown up with the belief that it was the mother's religion that determined the children's identity, since the Conservative Movement, like the greater Jewish community, accepted matrilineal descent. Interestingly, because Bonnie now considers herself a Reform Jew, that particular issue is of less importance; Reform Judaism, having voted to accept patrilineal descent in 1983, considers children of either a Jewish mother or a Jewish father to be Jewish if they are deliberately raised as Jews.

A friend of mine recently asked me how I decided to give this "gift" to my wife. She wanted to know what were the factors that made this the right choice. I had a hard time answering that one. I finally said that, technically speaking, there wasn't one thing per se that did it. Nothing forced us to decide one way or the other. The only criterion that we had was that we both had to be happy with the resolution. There is no right or wrong answer.

I had come to terms with my exact feelings on my religion. I was still Protestant, and I was secure in my identity. I had always been accepting of different religions and their beliefs. Here I was about to marry someone who did not share all of my viewpoints. I was fine with that. It dawned on me that if I were to love and respect this person with whom I was about to spend the rest of my life, I could certainly feel the same way toward my children. We would be one family. It no longer made sense to me that tolerance could apply to only one member. It somehow just *felt* right. Today, as we raise our two Jewish daughters, it still does.

Postscript

Talking about how you will raise children in an interfaith relationship definitely puts your communication skills to the test. Share your feelings with each other—don't be afraid to talk about what you need, and listen to what your partner needs. These needs are quite complex, usually built on years of one's own family religious experiences. Be aware that negative family experiences, even a lack of family experiences, shape these needs deeply as well. Many interfaith couples focus on what they think their future children may need and forget to talk about what they need from their own faith and religious traditions. If you as a couple can talk about what religious rituals you each need and why, then you can communicate about just about anything that will come up in your relationship.

The complexity of meeting one's personal needs is demonstrated by Paul and Marcia. Marcia, who was Jewish, felt deeply tied to her Jewish identity but had very few memories of family religious experiences from her childhood. Marcia's mother had died when she was a young girl, and from that time on they no longer celebrated Jewish rituals. She wanted to give her children the fond family memories she had lost as a child.

Paul was raised Protestant in a family that had had many religious traditions—regular church attendance, Sunday dinners, wonderful holiday celebrations, and grace before meals. Paul remembered these family traditions with much fondness but felt he was no longer connected to the "faith" aspects of his religious upbringing.

When Paul and Marcia expressed their own needs for religious traditions in their family, they both had a strong need to create shared family rituals. Paul wanted to commit to using religious rituals to bond their family together, creating the strong family memories for their children that he had had growing up. Paul felt he could raise his children within Judaism as long as they, as parents, re-created many shared family traditions he loved— including regular worship attendance, Shabbat dinners, joyous holidays, and blessings before meals. Paul wanted to give Marcia the gift of raising children in her Jewish faith because he realized that she had lost so much when her mother had died. Marcia was tremendously appreciative of Paul's support, asking him for his help in creating these special family moments built around their commitment to raise children within Judaism. Because Paul and Marcia focused on what they needed for themselves religiously, rather than trying to imagine what their future children would need, they were able to feel good about the decisions they made regarding their children's religious upbringing.

P. B.

5

You're Raising Them What? Telling My Parents We're Raising Jewish Kids

As a Protestant, I always assumed that one day I'd be taking my future kids to Sunday school. I also thought that I'd be teaching my future son to play baseball. As it turns out, though, I take my kids to shul (Yiddish for "school"—more specifically, the synagogue). It also happens that my kids are daughters, and I take them to ballet! Life throws you unexpected curveballs, and you deal with it. Now that I actually have a family of my own, I feel blessed to have two wonderful girls. The decision to raise them in the Jewish faith was not an easy one, but it's one I don't regret. What was equally hard was telling my parents.

Telling my in-laws was easy. After all, they're Jewish. Even though I did not convert, I think they felt fairly comfortable knowing that I would make every effort to help my wife teach the kids the Jewish faith and traditions. Telling *my* parents would be a different story. What on earth would I say? How would I broach the subject? What would their reaction be? Would they disapprove? Would they disown me?

Fortunately, my parents have always been loving and supportive, so I didn't think they would do anything rash. However, these thoughts did go through my mind, because this was alien territory for them as well. Many interfaith families *are* faced with strong disapproval from their parents when the news is broken. We've all heard the stories, and we've read the books. We may even know someone who's had problems. That someone could have been me!

No matter how open your parents are, there are some talks you have to be well prepared for if you want them to go right. My wife and I went over and over our reasons for raising the kids Jewish: We wanted to raise them in one faith so as not to confuse them. Also, because their mother is Jewish, and from a traditional Conservative background, they would be considered Jewish at the Conservative synagogue where Bonnie was then a member. However, we wanted to teach them about Christianity, my religion, to enrich their lives and give them an understanding of their heritage. They would still be allowed to "help" their Protestant grandparents and me celebrate Christmas and Easter. However, they would know that, bottom line, they are Jewish. Also, it would be really nice if my Protestant parents helped my children celebrate Jewish holidays like Shabbat, Sukkot, and Chanukah.

This was great in theory, but how would it work when we actually told my parents face to face? (I want to emphasize "face to face." This is not something you want to do over the phone, if possible.) If they gave us any argument or grief, we had to be prepared to tell them that it was important to us that they respect our decision. In addition, we needed to say that we'd put a lot of thought into it, we felt it's best for the kids, and most of all, we really wanted them to be included in the raising of our children.

That last part is what really helps you over the hump. It's crucial to let your parents know that you still want them to help and be involved. You want them every bit as active as they would have been had you decided to raise the kids as Christians. This lets them know that they are needed. Obviously, they won't know very much about the Jewish holidays and life-cycle events, but you can teach them. And in turn, they can participate. Just their being there is important. The Protestant grandparents can come over for a Shabbat dinner. They can assist in putting up the sukkah. They can play dreidel for chocolate gelt (or in our family, jelly beans) on Chanukah.

As it turns out, we had "the talk" one evening over dinner at my parents' house. It was a little nerve-racking trying to find a way to bring it up, but somehow we managed to find the courage. My mom was talking about Christmas stockings.

"Someday, when you two have kids, we have to remember to tell Aunt Ann to make them stockings," she said.

"Uh, well, Mom, Dad, we'd like to discuss that with you a little bit. You see, about Christmas . . ." They didn't say too much while we explained our plan—they just let us talk. However, when we got to the part about how much we hoped they would help us, they finally spoke.

"We'd love to help," they said.

Huh? You mean, that's it? No arguments? No grief? Of course, it wasn't that simple—it never is. They still had their questions to ask. For instance, they wanted to know what to do about Santa. And every once in a while, we have to tell them that "we prefer to do things such and such a way."

They may have had an inkling from our previous four years of dating and engagement that we'd choose this route. But, they hadn't been through the details of it like my wife and I had. My mother was very concerned that our children might go around telling their Protestant cousins that there's no such thing as Santa Claus. We in turn explained how our kids would help them celebrate the Christian holidays. We used an analogy of a birthday party. When you go to another person's birthday party, you are helping her celebrate *her* birthday. It isn't *your* birthday, but you can still have a piece of cake. You may also receive a goody bag to take home.

I also know that my mother, even today, feels a little uncertain when it comes to how she should approach religion with the kids. She has admitted to me that she is uncomfortable talking about baby Jesus in the manger. She doesn't quite know what we want her to say to our kids, or even if it's appropriate to talk about Jesus in the first place. I reassured her that, when explaining her Christianity, she may say anything that she normally believes. She should feel safe demonstrating her religion, in her own home, the way she has always practiced it. But, in order to not go overboard, I suggested that it wouldn't be appropriate to talk about it as if it was something our children should believe in, too. She gave me a look that said, "Well, duh." At that moment I knew it would be all right. She may be a little disappointed that she's in this position. I'm sure she's always had visions of teaching her grandkids the Bible stories that she taught me. And there are times when I can tell that she wants to go all out with our kids at Christmastime. Somehow, though, she manages to restrain herself. With our continued guidance, I think that she has adjusted fairly well, considering.

For my dad, his biggest worry was that, in focusing on Judaism with my kids, somehow I would lose sight of my Protestant traditions and background. I'm sure that he would love me no matter what I did, but it's got to be hard on a parent to think that his child would turn his back on so many years of upbringing. I reassured him that this was something that I would not and could not ever forget. As he watches us raise our family today, I know he feels good about how we haven't neglected to have our kids help me celebrate my holidays. This is evident in the fact that he and my mom really get into helping my family celebrate Jewish traditions. They gladly come to our annual Chanukah party, they attend Shabbat dinners with us at the Jewish Community Center, and they even smothered their granddaughters with hugs and kisses on the day of their religious school consecrations. I think they would be less cooperative if they weren't comfortable with our methods.

All in all, they were, and still are, supportive of our plan to raise our kids Jewish. I don't know if it was the part about including them, or the fact that they wouldn't have to share us with my in-laws on Christmas and Easter! But my wife and I are extremely lucky to have parents who are understanding and want to help.

I'm not naive enough to think that this is the norm. Many parents facing the idea of their child marrying someone of a different faith are going to have stronger issues in seeing their grandchildren raised in a different culture and religion. It's important to recognize and respect your parents' concerns. They have preconceived notions about your children and their role in your children's lives, just as you do. Hopefully, over time, and with a lot of coaching and conversation, you can get to a point where your biggest problem is trying to keep your dad from eating all the coconut-flavored jelly beans at Chanukah.

Postscript

Many couples avoid making a decision about the religious identity of their children simply because they do not wish to hurt one set of parents. Soon after their engagement, Mandy and John made a decision to raise their future children within Judaism but then decided they would not tell John's Catholic parents, fearing that John's mother, a very devout Catholic, would be terribly disappointed. Mandy and John decided not to tell Mandy's parents either, even though Mandy felt her parents would be thrilled that their Judaism would be passed on to their grandchildren. If John's or Mandy's parents asked whether they had made a decision about the grandchildren, their game plan was to say, "We have not yet decided."

Their silence about the decision as their wedding day approached left both sets of parents wondering if their adult children cared enough about their religious traditions to pass a faith on to their future grandchildren. Without telling Mandy or John, their mothers talked with each other, sharing their mutual heartache and opting to confront their children with their shared concern that their grandchildren would have no religion.

When confronted, Mandy and John initially stuck with their "we have not yet decided" response. Finally, their tearful mothers shared their anxiety, with each mother saying that they would rather have their grandchildren raised in one faith tradition than no faith or no decision made about a faith. In shock, John and Mandy conferred with each other and told their parents that they had indeed made a decision to raise the children Jewish. John's parents were more relieved than disappointed, and Mandy's parents, happy that a decision had been made, felt empathetic with their Catholic in-laws.

In hindsight, John and Mandy would now say that it's important to let your parents in on what you have decided sooner rather than later. Both sets of parents now gather with Mandy and John to celebrate holidays. Mandy's Jewish parents have accompanied John and his family for Midnight Mass on Christmas Eve and have come to John's extended family's Catholic life-cycle rituals, including baptisms when new cousins were born. Both mothers enjoy making lots of matzah balls together for the annual Passover seder, to which all of John's family is always invited.

P. B.

Part II

NEGOTIATING
LIFE-CYCLE
EVENTS

6

When Nothing Else Will Do, Have a "Jewish-ish" Wedding

After determining what religion our children would have, it was time to set our sights on the wedding itself. Planning any wedding can be tough. When you're planning an interfaith wedding, however, "tough" is just a starting point. In our case, we had the pleasure of appeasing the usual wishes of both of our families (which guests to invite, who should accompany whom down the aisle, seating charts, and so on), but on top of it all, Bonnie and I had to decide if we were going to have a Protestant ceremony or a Jewish one.

Looking back, the first issue we ran into was trying not to offend any member of either family. My parents had their own visions of how a proper wedding should take place. These were probably ideas that had been cooking in their heads for years. Basically, Protestant weddings are plain and simple. There is no "Protestant culture" that is an integral part of the ceremony or reception (unless you count the garter toss). You walk down the aisle, a minister marries the bride and groom, maybe a song or poem is included, you walk back up the aisle, and then there is a party afterward.

In the Jewish wedding, however, there are countless Jewish traditions, many of which Bonnie's parents considered important. For instance, you've got the *chuppah* under which the couple are married, the breaking of the glass, the blessing over the wine, the blessing over the challah, and dancing the hora. Bonnie and I had the task of somehow trying to make sure nobody felt uncomfortable on our special day.

"*Our* special day." We almost forgot. Somewhere along the way, we remembered that it was important for us to make sure our day went the way *we* wanted it to go. Don't get me wrong. Our parents were very cooperative and had only our best interests at heart. But we were the only two people who could plan our wedding the way we wanted it to be.

Exactly what did we want? "Boy, that's a good question," we wondered. "We've never done one of these." We started by making a list of all the things that were important to us. Bonnie had been to many of her cousins' Jewish weddings and was accustomed to seeing the traditional Jewish elements that I mentioned earlier. She had always felt that these features would be there when she herself became a bride. These traditions were totally foreign to me and made me nervous that my side of the family would feel completely lost and neglected.

Because I'm a typical guy, I never really thought much about weddings. I hadn't even been to that many, let alone a Jewish wedding. There weren't any burning Protestant cultural items that I just had to have. Although I'm of Scottish descent, I felt that kilts would be a little too much for her family to take. So you can pretty much guess how I felt about the flower arrangements and dessert menus.

Between the two of us, however, there was one thing about which we both had strong feelings. We both wanted to have God as part of our ceremony. After all, God is a big part of our lives. So would we have a minister marry us? What about a rabbi? Given our feelings about our faiths, either of those choices wouldn't be fair to one of us. Bonnie said that having a minister perform the ritual would make her feel that it was a Protestant wedding. Likewise, a rabbi would give the service an overly Jewish tone for me. Although we had decided that we would raise our children Jewish, we still couldn't have a Jewish wedding. For this, all our Jewish family and friends told us, you need both the bride and groom to be Jewish. It wasn't until later that I learned there are some rabbis who will officiate at a wedding where one partner isn't Jewish. But even if I had known that at the time, it wouldn't have been the right decision for us.

How about a co-officiated wedding? I think the word "officiated" is very appropriate. With all the negotiating we were doing, I expected a guy in a black and white striped shirt and yellow flag to marry us. It would be hard to find two clergy who would agree to jointly conduct a wedding service. There aren't many out there who see their role in conducting an intermarriage wedding as proper. Although we felt that we could eventually find the right two people, we decided that this approach didn't make us comfortable. With the ceremony divided into a Jewish part and a Christian part, we just couldn't envision there being any flow to the service. It may work for some couples, but it was not our style. Then there was the issue of where to hold the wedding. For the same reasons, we didn't feel it would be fair to one of us if the ceremony were held in either a church or synagogue.

We could see why everyone told us that interfaith marriages were difficult. Sometimes it crossed our minds that we had to be crazy to even attempt such a feat, but our love for each other kept us determined. Then one day, we found the perfect solution. A friend of Bonnie's mom, named Sheila, was a justice of the peace who performed civil ceremonies. She also happened to be a cantor, the person who leads the synagogue services in song. She specialized in officiating at weddings between interfaith couples and happily agreed to involve God in the wedding service. As a bonus, she was able to perform the songs in our wedding.

Sheila suggested that a nice hotel would be a warm and friendly neutral location to hold the service. This worked out extremely well for the reception, too. We were able to incorporate some Jewish elements, such as the *chuppah* and the breaking of the glass. We even danced to a traditional Jewish tune called the *freilach* at the reception. I was worried that my Protestant friends and family would be lost, but to my surprise, this dance really energized the crowd and set a festive tone for the rest of the afternoon. Because these were mostly cultural and not religious details, my family did not feel threatened. As much as it was important that Bonnie and I planned the wedding based on our tastes, these are family affairs, and everyone should be made to feel as welcome as possible.

Having figured out the *how* and the *where*, we were faced with the question of *who* would show up. Many of my wife's relatives were Orthodox and did not approve of our marriage. Her great-uncle, for example, politely declined our invitation. At first, I was upset—no, angry. I thought it was insulting. After having thought about it for a few days, however, I came to understand his position. Her great-uncle was deeply rooted in his faith, which told him that intermarriage was not appropriate. Although we'd miss him, I now had a sudden respect for the man who stood for what he thought was right.

More importantly, Bonnie's grandmother was riding the fence as to whether she would attend or not. To Bonnie, a wedding without her *bubba* would be like apples without honey on Rosh HaShanah, only on a much bigger scale. Ever since my wife had broken the news to her grandmother that we were getting married, Bubba had said that she wished her well but was not sure she would come to the wedding. Again, at first I was upset about her response. Then as I cooled down, I was able to respect her beliefs. With Bubba, however, it was a different story than with Bonnie's great-uncle. I did not really know him. I did know her grandmother, though. And I knew how much it would crush Bonnie if Bubba were not there. By this time, my feelings had turned to ones of anxiety. This had become a big issue for me, too.

Fortunately, thanks to some heart-to-heart talks with Bonnie's stepmother, Bubba decided that what was most important was her granddaughter's happiness. She came to the wedding. She even danced with me that wonderful summer afternoon. And while the Bo Winiker Wedding Band played Benny Goodman's "Memories of You," I'll never forget what she said to me. "Jim, you're my grandson now."

Postscript

Julia and Mitchell, a newly engaged interfaith couple, set aside an evening to discuss their dreams for their wedding day. Before they began their discussion, they each made a list of all the things they considered most important—both during the ceremony and the reception. They then circled the three things on their list that were the most important to them. After that, Julia turned her paper over and made a list of all the things that she thought would be most important to Mitchell, and he did the same for her. At that point they discussed these lists, beginning with what each thought would be most important to their partner. The conversation enabled them to feel that they were sensitive to each other's needs. Julia and Mitchell talked about compromises each might be willing to make so that each of them could have two of their top three needs met on their wedding day.

Since they actually had fun doing this exercise and felt that they had really communicated well, they each proceeded to make another list of the things they thought were most important to each partner's parents/family. They discussed possible ways to meet at least one of each of their family's top needs. At the end of the evening, they were amazed at how far they had come planning a near-perfect wedding.

If you follow Julia and Mitchell's strategy, you may find that this discussion can also be an opportunity to learn about life-cycle rituals and traditions in your partner's faith and culture. Mitchell gained an understanding of both the Swedish and Lutheran traditions that Julia valued; she understood the elements of a Jewish ceremony that were important to Mitchell. They had separated out what they wanted for their wedding versus what their parents wanted but had found ways to enable both sets of parents to feel comfortable and involved. Julia and Mitchell ended their discussion with an expression of appreciation to each other, feeling that they had strengthened their communication and learned about their partner's needs by listening with love and caring.

P. B.

7

B'rit Milah or *B'rit Bat*?
How This Christian Dad Came to Give
His Daughters Hebrew Names

Once we had finally agreed on how we would raise our children, I began to grow comfortable with our decision.

"You know, they'll celebrate Chanukah, not Christmas," my wife stated.

"Sure," I replied with confidence.

"They're going to go to temple, not church."

"I would expect that."

"If we have a girl, she'll have a *b'rit bat*."

"That's the baby-naming ceremony, right? It'll be beautiful."

"If we have a boy, he'll have a *b'rit milah*."

"No probl . . . Wait. Isn't that where they cut the . . . ?"

"Mmmhmm."

We ended up having two girls. However, back then, I had no idea what we would have. To be honest, I spent a few moments pondering what I had gotten myself into. I had no problem with the idea of circumcision itself. I had been; why shouldn't my son be? It was just the idea of making a big deal out of the procedure that made me pause and wonder. In my imagination, I pictured all of our family and friends gathered in our living room, eating delicious food, engaging in lively conversation, and genuinely enjoying themselves. Then the mohel, who performs the ritual, steps up to the baby, pulls out his scissors, and SNIP! Bonnie's family shouts, "*Mazal tov!*" My family becomes silent—wide-eyed—frozen like deer in your headlights—then runs to the bathroom to recycle their sesame bagels.

What was I going to do? I finally decided that a commitment was a commitment. My wife and I had made our decision together, and we would stick to it. If we had boys, we would just have to ease my family into the idea of the *b'rit milah*, or bris as it is often called.

When joining two families of different faiths together, nothing else screams, "Welcome to intermarriage!" quite like a *b'rit milah*. Fortunately, my family has been very supportive every step of the way, and I'm sure they'd have behaved just fine if we had had a son. My guess was that they would have been so overjoyed just to have a grandson to love (and spoil) that nothing else would have mattered.

As it turns out, God has yet to test us on our reactions to a bris. Instead, God has given Bonnie and me two beautiful girls, for whom we had baby namings. While no surgery is involved during this ceremony, a *b'rit bat* is still a uniquely Jewish moment that can be foreign to a Protestant family, such as mine. Interestingly, it can be new to many American Jews, as well, for the types of ceremonies in which Jewish baby girls are named today are elaborations on the way girls were generally named in past generations.

The first time I ever heard of a baby naming, I thought, "What's the deal with that? Didn't the parents already name her at the hospital? Why do they have to name her again?" As my wife explained, this is to give the daughter her Hebrew name. She also said that because today's baby namings are outgrowths of an older, more simple ritual, there is a lot of flexibility regarding what we could do for a ceremony. If we had had a boy and a *b'rit milah*, there would have been plenty of precedent to follow. Although, the only part that is commanded in the Torah is the circumcision, a bris has many long-standing traditions. On the other hand, there are no steadfast rules for celebrating the birth of a daughter. The baby namings of previous generations were simple ceremonies at the synagogue and usually did not involve the female members of the family. Today's *b'rit bat* in America has evolved into a celebration that includes the whole family. It can be held in the home or in the synagogue. In our case, we chose to have the baby naming in our home, so my family would feel more comfortable.

Before our daughter was born, we had decided what all her names were to be and after whom she would be named. We knew that we wanted to incorporate the names of our grandmothers, who had recently passed away. My wife told me that it is customary for Ashkenazic, or Eastern European, Jews to name their children after a deceased member of the family as a way of remembering them.

"Ah, that's why you don't see a lot of 'Juniors' in Jewish boys' names," I surmised. But wait a minute, we could have a problem.

"What about when you want to name your child after someone with a name that's, let's just say, no longer in style—like your grandmother, Gertrude?" I asked.

"Or your grandmother, Mildred?" she added.

"Yeah, I don't want her to get beaten up at school, or called 'Mildew.'"

Bonnie explained that it is a common custom in the United States for families to use just the first letter of the ancestor's Hebrew name. She said, "Gertrude's 'Hebrew' name was Gittel (which is actually Yiddish). So for our daughter, we could take the 'G' from Gittel to make Gabrielle for the English name."

"Oh, so it's a loophole!" I replied.

For our second daughter, we used this "loophole" again and named her Molly, after my grandma Mildred. For the Hebrew name we chose Chava, which means "life" or "lively" (turns out we were more than right with this one) and is the Hebrew equivalent of Eve. I'm sure if my grandma had been Jewish, this would have been *her* Hebrew name. This was also a nice opportunity to give Molly a

Hebrew name belonging to another one of my wife's grandmothers. We felt it would be more appropriate to use this existing Hebrew name, rather than make one up for the name Molly. Bottom line, I learned that there are a lot of acceptable ways to come up with names in the Jewish tradition.

The order of events for the baby namings of our two daughters went something like this: Friends and family arrived at our home and began to mingle, while waiting for the rabbi to begin. At noon, the rabbi was ready to start. But some of *my* family and friends weren't there yet. They were, as usual, sociably late! We had forgotten to tell them that this is one occasion where it is not fashionable to be tardy.

Because it was a learning experience for many of the guests who attended our daughters' baby namings, I think that most were fascinated by them. The rabbi who came to our home to perform the ceremony did an excellent job of explaining what was about to take place. After welcoming all of our friends and family, he told everyone the significance of the baby naming. This was great for both Christians and Jews who had never witnessed one before. After my parents carried our daughter into the room, the rabbi gave her the Hebrew name we had selected. He then led us in a prayer that thanked God for sustaining us and bringing us to this moment. This prayer, known as the *Shehecheyanu*, is said at many Jewish get-togethers. The rabbi then had us all say the blessing for daughters: "May God make you as Sarah, Rebekah, Rachel, and Leah." Since these blessings were spoken in Hebrew, he fortunately made them repeat-after-me prayers. He then gave us the English translations. The rabbi concluded with a blessing that recognized that our daughter was entering the covenant with God and that our hopes were for her to love learning through study of the Torah, be happy, be respectful, and act in honest and ethical ways.

One of my worst fears, when we informed my parents that we would raise our children Jewish, was that they would say, "That's fine; just not too Jewish." Having a rabbi hold your daughter and pray that she would study Torah can be a little overwhelming for a Christian dad hearing it for the first time. I doubt that it's something a Christian grandparent experiences every day, either. This was definitely our first test. Happily, my parents were eagerly engaged in the ceremony, joyful just to be part of their granddaughter's life.

When the rabbi finished, my in-laws said the blessings over the wine and challah. The participation of both sets of grandparents was not only beautiful, but also crucial. Bonnie and I had coordinated what would take place ahead of time. We wanted to make sure that both families felt at home and comfortable with the ceremony. By having Bonnie's parents say the blessings and my parents carry our daughter into the room, everyone was a part of the baby naming.

Nothing but smiles adorned the faces of those who were in our living room on both of those occasions. Instead of potentially alienating my family, the baby namings resoundingly opened the door and welcomed them into our daughters' Jewish faith. Looking back, I think that my wife and I were the only ones who were nervous. During our first daughter's ceremony, I remember not wanting to mess up. I could just hear my Jewish in-laws: "there he goes messing up one of our fine traditions." (For the record, though, I don't really believe anyone would have thought that.)

After the rabbi gave our daughters their names, my wife and I each wanted to say a few words about why we chose these names, the people after whom we had named them, and what their Hebrew names meant to us. In both ceremonies though, Bonnie was too emotional to speak, so it was up to me to do the talking. I began by telling everyone about the meanings these names had for us and how we hoped our daughters could emulate their loving great-grandmothers. I felt much more confident for my second daughter's naming three years later. You should have heard me pronounce "Chava!"

After the ceremony, it was, of course, time to enjoy the delicious spread of food covering the dining room table. Bagels, lox, pastries, cheeses, noodle kugel—you name it, we ate it. Like most Jewish get-togethers, it just wouldn't be official without the food. Everyone was laughing, talking, and eating. I didn't care that it was thirty degrees and snowing outside. As far as I was concerned, it was a gorgeous day.

I'm sure that if we had had boys, each *b'rit milah* would have been just as fulfilling. Right now, though, I'm just as happy letting my friends with boys have the honors.

I'll never forget either of our daughters' baby namings, but the first one struck me as incredibly significant. The days leading up to the *b'rit bat* were a little nerve-racking for me. This was really it—the commencement of raising our daughter in Judaism. I was about to give her a type of name that I did not have. Was I going to feel connected to my wife and child? Then, I realized: this was *my* daughter. She was a part of *me*. On the day of the baby naming, it all came together for me. There I was, standing in my living room, a Christian, in the middle of a Jewish ceremony expounding on these Hebrew names. I looked out at the room full of loved ones. I looked down at my daughter's sweet face. I couldn't have felt more at home.

Postscript

Choosing a Hebrew name for our children is a way of honoring or memorializing loved ones. While the Hebrew names accomplish this, they have an additional—even deeper—significance. The names are, in actuality, covenant names*. By bestowing a Hebrew name on a child, that child is formally entered into the covenant between God and the Jewish people. If you can discuss this openly with non-Jewish grandparents beforehand and give them a sense of what to expect, they will most likely be more comfortable. They would not be surprised, then, to hear the hope expressed that the child will engage in Torah study.*

Equally important is reassuring the grandparents of another faith that you want them to have a strong connection to their grandchildren. Stress the special things that you hope they will be able to teach and pass on to the children. It may be hard for them to hear that this won't include some of the religious rituals or traditions that they passed on to you, but emphasize all the other things that you hope they will pass on, such as their values. In addition, there are roles in a baby-naming, b'rit bat, *or* b'rit milah *ceremony that would be appropriate for grandparents of another faith. Talk to the officiant about how to include both sets of grandparents and any other important family members from both sides. This is a way to honor them and publicly state your hope that they will play a key role in your child's life.*

Regarding the b'rit milah *ceremony, in reality most people attending have some level of discomfort. Some people have strong and even divisive opinions on whether or not circumcision is necessary, and there is no lack of research to support both sides of the argument. For Jews, though, circumcision isn't primarily about health. It is first and foremost a covenantal and spiritual act that connects the baby to thousands of years of tradition. That is the power and beauty of circumcision. No parent of any faith enjoys the moment of the circumcision, but there is some comfort to be gained in knowing that the* mohel/et *performing the ritual is a specialist who does this day in and day out, and that this is an act that has been performed generation after generation. Some of the discomfort is because those of us outside of the health care professions are not accustomed to watching surgery live and in real time. Here's a thought to put everyone at ease: remind guests that only one person in the room must keep his/her eyes open, and that's the* mohel/et *performing the circumcision!*

S. E.

8

Losing a Loved One

Thankfully, neither Bonnie nor I have yet lost a loved one in our immediate family. Just because death has not entered our household yet, however, doesn't mean that we haven't talked about it. It's not like we're obsessed with the subject, but we do feel it necessary to have a plan. You never know when exactly you're going to have to "make arrangements." When the day comes, what will we do?

The Jewish and Christian faiths have different rituals for dealing with death. For interfaith families, there is no well-established precedent. After she's gone, it's awfully hard to ask your spouse, "Do you want the rabbi to perform your eulogy?" Or, "How do you want us to mourn for you?" Or to find out, "I always expected that we'd be laid to rest where my grandparents are. I didn't know it was a Christian cemetery."

There are so many details to figure out that it does no good to wait until it's too late. It's like having a will—it's depressing to have to think about it, but it's got to be done. Talk about it, even put your thoughts to paper, get it over with, and then you don't have to worry about it—the matter is settled.

In stark contrast, if you take a look at weddings, details are often imagined even before people are engaged. Many young people have dreamed about how every aspect of their wedding would turn out. They always wanted an outdoor wedding, or they really had their hearts set on being married at sea on a cruise. They'd serve white chocolate desserts shaped like swans, smothered with raspberry sauce, or have a big barbeque on the lawn. But when it comes to death, funerals, and mourning, many people don't take the time to plan ahead. Why? Let's face it—it's not exactly a fun subject to dream about.

For couples who share the same faith, planning ahead is important, but many of the rituals are well-established, according to their religion. Although it doesn't prevent disagreements on what to do when a loved one dies, people have a general picture of what to expect. They'll be buried in a Jewish cemetery. The immediate family will sit shivah (the Jewish period of mourning). For some Christians, there will be an open-casket viewing (something not done by Jews). Or there will be a traditional Irish wake, or whatever is the family's custom.

The interfaith couple, on the other hand, cannot afford to leave the details to chance. Just like the other life-cycle events that they had so meticulously planned out, making sure that both religions were considered, that both sets of in-laws were accommodated, that the moment reflected their dual-faith lifestyle in a consistent manner, the interfaith couple must be ready for the last of the life-cycle events—death.

Bonnie and I felt that, as painful as it was to think about, we needed to consider what we would do. Where would be the best place for burial that would accept Christians and Jews? Is cremation an option? Would I, the Christian, want to sit shivah for her? If something happened to us while our children were young, who would take them in? Would they continue to be raised Jewish? As we get older, our specifics may change, but we knew that we had to start discussing the framework now. The first thing we needed to do was to understand what our religious traditions expected of us.

To compare to weddings again, I've noticed that Protestant funerals are often of the same structure as our weddings—loose. There are a few traditions to follow, but generally speaking, the procedures are basic. Most of the time, there is a reception or viewing at the funeral home. Usually a day later, there is a funeral service at the funeral home or church. There is no standard time frame in which to hold these.

During the Protestant service, someone, usually a minister, friend, or family member, performs the eulogy, or remembrance. This is a speech to celebrate the life of the deceased, to speak of him or her in an upbeat way, and to provide comfort for the grieving. Sometimes, more than one person gives a remembrance. Prayers are recited, including the Lord's Prayer. Often, a hymn or two are sung.

After the funeral service, a procession is led to the cemetery or other resting place, for the final committal. Most often, the minister says a few more words, including the recitation of a traditional psalm. Another prayer is said. Then, the grieving friends and family retreat to the funeral parlor or home of the deceased for a reception. At the cemetery, the casket is sometimes lowered into the ground after the family leaves. Sometimes it is lowered while everyone is still gathered.

The Jewish practice is somewhat similar, but with different prayers and a few extra traditions. One big difference is that Jewish law requires that the body be buried within twenty-four hours, or as soon as possible after that. (Protestants often will wait longer to bury.) Just before the funeral service, the immediate family "cuts k'riah." This is the symbolic tearing of clothes representing the tear in their lives caused by the death of the loved one. Generally, the funeral home will provide a black ribbon to cut as a substitute. Many Jews also wish to be buried covered in a shroud. Jewish families traditionally choose a plain pine box, or at least a wooden casket instead of something more elaborate.

There is no set liturgy for a Jewish service, though a selection of psalms are recited. The rabbi is often the one who gives the eulogy, or *hespeid*, as it is called in Hebrew, although sometimes family members or friends do it. A Jewish service will also often include poems or meditative readings. The service ends with the chanting of *El Malei Rachamim*—a prayer asking God to give rest to the soul. Then everyone proceeds to the burial site. After additional readings, and once the casket has been lowered, the Mourner's *Kaddish* is recited.

Jewish and Protestant funeral procedures are both basic. They have a minimum number of rules that need to be observed. Where the big difference lies between the two is in the numerous customs that surround Jewish death and mourning. Many of the traditions that I have mentioned originate from traditional practices and are modified or reinterpreted by Conservative or Reform Jews. Take, for instance, cutting *k'riah*. Some Orthodox Jews will cut their actual clothes. Most Reform Jews cut a black ribbon and pin it to their clothes. Either way, the ritual is considered fulfilled.

When Bonnie's grandmother in Rhode Island passed away a few years ago, we observed and participated in many of these traditional rituals. After her casket was lowered into the ground, we each took a turn with the shovel, throwing dirt into the grave in a symbolic act of closure, seen by Jewish tradition as a final act of caring for the dead.

When we returned from the cemetery, we all washed our hands—not because they were dirty from shoveling, but because we were taking part in another tradition. This one grows out of super-stition and has different meanings to different people. For us, it was to wash our hands of any impurity connected to the cemetery or death itself.

Back at her grandmother's house, I noticed that all of the mirrors were covered. Bonnie explained to me that this was so that people wouldn't be tempted to peer into them to see how they looked. It is a traditional custom for those in mourning to not shave or put on makeup, another aspect of not thinking about one's appearance. There are also ancient superstitions associated with covering the mirrors. Today many Jews leave their mirrors uncovered, because they view the tradition as unnecessary or archaic.

For seven days, her father sat shivah in his mother's house. I found it incredibly therapeutic to be able to mourn with family and friends for more than just one day. Sure, most people grieve for a long time, but to actually have a tradition to follow for a set period of days was comforting. We received extended family and well-wishers throughout the week. They brought lots of food and conversation. It was also beautiful to witness how many people cared for Bubba.

Bonnie took part in each of these traditions. This is how she was raised. This is what she is used to. These practices have helped her and her parents grieve in years past.

She and I have talked about how sitting shivah would be a helpful process for our family. If I pass away first, she and our daughters would sit shivah for me, even though I am Christian and will probably have a ceremony that recognizes that in some way. In mourning, I'd expect my wife and daughters to follow any of the Jewish customs and laws that they wanted. They will be the ones grieving, not me. If she passes away first, I expect that I would sit shivah with Gabby and Molly for their mother. We have made a commitment to have a Jewish home. These are Jewish traditions that are designed to help the grieving. My side of the family would be more than welcome to participate, but would also be allowed to grieve in any manner in which they feel comfortable.

I imagine that my family would see the beauty in these Jewish rituals, laws, and customs of mourning, just as I have come to appreciate them. They are designed to comfort the grieving friends and family. I also expect that when my Christian parents pass away, my wife, daughters, and I will grieve together in a very Jewish way. Sometimes, during a period of great stress, it's hard to play things by ear. It's nice to know what you are expected to do.

I find that the timeline provided by the stages of the Jewish mourning process are psychologically uplifting. Shivah is for seven days—no more. After that, you are expected to start coming out of the house and getting on with life. Another part of Jewish mourning is the thirty-day period of *sh'loshim*. This includes the first seven days (shivah) and twenty-three more. During those twenty-three days, the grieving family slowly reacclimatizes itself back into the world outside of the house. The family is still expected to recite *Kaddish* daily but is allowed to return to work. Getting out and meeting with people is encouraged, as long as it is not a party, entertainment function, or sporting event.

Before the end of the first year, the family may have an "unveiling." This is a Jewish-American custom of holding a religious ceremony at the cemetery to unveil the deceased's gravestone. Remembering the one-year mark of the person's death is referred to as *yahrzeit*. It is observed annually by saying *Kaddish* and lighting a *yahrzeit* candle, which burns for twenty-four hours.

These Jewish customs help the family in times of emotional stress, without letting them wallow in a morbid atmosphere. They slowly encourage the mourners to reenter the world of the living, while still honoring the memory of their departed loved one.

How it all actually works out for us remains to be seen. But at least Bonnie and I have started the ball rolling. Talking to our clergy has also been helpful. If nothing else, making the appointments to see the rabbi and minister provided initiative and an abundance of information as to what our options are—especially regarding the services and cemetery restrictions. We were relieved to find out that the rabbi and minister were open to working with our unique needs. Both have dealt with interfaith families like ours. They have given us numerous ideas about what to do when the day comes. But most of all, they have let us know that they care and will help us.

Postscript

One of the most difficult end-of-life decisions people must make is where to be buried. Will we be buried in a family plot? If so, whose family plot—the husband's or the wife's? Would the Jewish partner be comfortable being buried in a cemetery where there are symbols of another faith? How will the Christian partner feel about being buried in a Jewish cemetery that does not permit the placing of a cross on the grave marker? These are all issues that need to be discussed openly and honestly.

As difficult as it may be to discuss, it is helpful to sit down together and draw up some plans. Think through different scenarios. What would you want for yourself should you predecease your spouse? What would you be comfortable doing for your spouse and for yourself if you were the surviving spouse? And what do you think would be necessary and/or appropriate for your children?

You need to be sensitive, too, to the feelings of family members. For instance, how will the Christian family feel about Jewish rituals that the Jewish family may observe to mourn their Christian relative? Once the decisions have been reached concerning funeral and mourning rituals, it is important to inform the families what the plan is. This will help avoid potential misunderstanding and extra pain at the time when the plan will have to be put into effect. These are sometimes difficult conversations, but avoiding the issues only makes for more difficulty.

S. E.

Part III

PARENTING

9

Questions about God
from the Backseat

"Daddy, you know everything, don't you?" is something you would think a guy likes to hear from his kids. At first, my head swelled to fill the interior of the minivan I was driving on the way to preschool. Gabby, then five years old, had just floated this softball of a statement as a distraction to catch me off guard for what she really wanted to ask.

As I tried to explain to her that, while I do know a lot, I do not know everything, she couldn't wait to interrupt me with her first question.

"Daddy, when does water become ice?"

"When the temperature gets to thirty-two degrees or colder, the water freezes to form ice."

"Daddy, why are leaves green?"

"Well, that's because they're full of chlorophyll, which is used by the tree to convert sunlight into food." ("This is easy. Maybe I do know everything," I thought.)

Then came the sneak attack. "Daddy, what is God?"

As I fumbled my way through the best impromptu answer I could think of, I couldn't help but wish that my wife were there to help me field this one. My daughter had suddenly become the press corps, and I was the White House press secretary.

I knew that whatever I told her needed to be good because she would take this information and use it as a building block to form her images of God and her Jewish religion. I was worried that if I gave the wrong answer, I could give her a warped sense of what or who God is. Or worse, I could turn her away from religion and a belief in God forever. Where was my parenting manual when I needed it?

To top it all off, I, as the Christian parent of the family, had to give my daughter an explanation that would be satisfactory according to Judaism. In addition, it would have to meet her mother's own image of God. My wife and I had never really discussed the topic of how we would explain God to our kids. Our many discussions about how to raise children in an interfaith family had not prepared me for this very moment.

I had probably envisioned Gabby, at a much older age, scheduling an appointment to see my wife and me to discuss the meaning of God. "Mom, Dad? I want to have a chat about God with you. How's next Tuesday at 9:30 sound?" This would have given us plenty of time to prepare our answer. Then we could have presented a united front with a consistent message. Unfortunately, at that moment in the minivan, in the middle of traffic on Eisenhower Parkway, I had to hope that what I told Gabby, without any preparation, was not only correct, but also what her mother would have wanted her to hear.

At least I had made the decision to tell my daughter something that would be consistent with her faith and not mine. I had decided that it would not be appropriate to try and discuss my belief in Jesus and how He relates to God. If there's one thing that my wife and I had previously agreed upon, it was to make sure that our daughters received a Jewish education and knew that they were not both

Jewish and Christian. One day, they're going to be curious and ask me about my religion, and I'll tell them. After all, the more they know about other religions, the more educated and tolerant they'll be.

Fortunately, my wife and I have always believed the Judeo-Christian God to be the same God. From this viewpoint, I found it easier to simply relate my view of God, as my parents and ministers had taught me, and how I had molded my belief in God over the years. I had to laugh as I briefly thought of what an ancient Roman and Jewish interfaith family would have gone through. At least neither one of us was polytheistic! So, instead of focusing on the differences between Judaism and Christianity, I kept my discussion to the commonalities of our belief in God. "There is only one God. God is everywhere. God is a loving God." To which she replied, "Oh. Can we have ice cream tonight?"

In the end, I found the interfaith issue to not be as difficult as I thought it would be. What turned out to be the most challenging was taking a step back and examining my own view of God. While I have always believed in God, I haven't ever tried to explain the concept to anyone—especially a five-year-old, whom it was my duty to teach. Somehow I managed to find a way, and each day I get a little better at it.

I know that my daughter's religious education will not end with that one discussion we had in the car. It will continue throughout her life. In fact, since then, Gabby, her sister Molly, and I have had a few more talks about God. I have also taught them about my belief in Jesus. Surprisingly, they seem to be unfazed by it. Hopefully, that's due to a consistent Jewish message from their mother and me. They understand that they are Jewish, and their tradition believes one thing, whereas my Christian tradition believes something else. I find the experience of being part of their education refreshing and rewarding, not just in teaching them, but also in reaffirming my own belief in God.

Postscript

Talking about God is challenging for most parents and often even more challenging for parents from two different faith backgrounds. It helps to have discussions early on as a couple about the importance of religion in your life, long before your children are old enough to ask their own questions. Consider the classic story of the little boy who goes down the street to play with the slightly older new kid who has just moved in. Upon returning home, he asks his parents, "Where do I come from?" While they thought they had a year or two before they might have to deal with this question, it is obvious to them that the older boy has hastened the need for the talk. After the boy's parents go through a long explanation about the birds and the bees, the boy looks quizzically at his parent and says, "No, Johnny down the street comes from Cleveland. Where do I come from?"

There are no right or wrong answers, and what your children believe at age five will probably be very different from what they believe at age ten and different still from age fifteen. Rather than sharing factual information, God-talk opens up the opportunity for children to develop their own understanding of God. Though they may want to know what their parents think, one way to advance the conversation is to ask them what they believe. Children will often ask a question about a topic because they have an idea they want to share. When they ask about God, ask in return, "Tell me, what do you think about God?" This open-ended conversation may well open up a fruitful dialogue.

Speak honestly about your own beliefs, no matter how well developed or unresolved they may be. Expressing respect for the beliefs of your partner and your child is more important than having all the answers. It is fine, and can even be helpful, to show that you yourself have doubts or internal struggles about belief, but that you keep on asking the questions.

H. J.

10

Don't They Know I'm Jewish?
Our Children Start to Comprehend
Their Jewish Identity

I knew it was bound to happen. There was really no way to prevent it—not that I wanted to prevent it. What I'm referring to is the fact that our daughters' Jewish identities have started to come alive within them.

This thirst for knowledge has begun with Gabby, who, being older and attending religious school on Saturdays, asks questions and makes comments about her Jewish world that her mother and I haven't expected. More than once her queries have caused Bonnie and me to look at each other and ask, "You wanna handle this one?" Most of the time, though, we're able to sufficiently answer our girls with responses that make sense to them and are consistent with our interfaith philosophy. Later, when we're alone, Bonnie and I laugh hysterically at being caught off guard, or by the humorous way in which the girls opine on a subject.

Even though kids do say the darndest things, not all of their comments are funny. The pure innocence of their remarks can be refreshing. Sometimes, I feel their sorrow as they discover something about their Jewish identity that makes them feel sad.

For the past two Decembers, Gabby has begun to notice that most people in our neighborhood don't put menorahs in their windows. In fact, most of the trees in the yards of our street have Christmas lights. "Why are there so many Christmas lights? Where are the Chanukah decorations?" she asked.

Gabby's friend, Claire, who is also growing up in an interfaith family, uses the "light test" to determine who in her neighborhood is Jewish and who is Christian. "The houses with lights are the Christians, and the houses without lights are the Jews."

Claire's mom laughed as she told me how she tried to explain to Claire that that isn't always the case. "Unfortunately, it has given my daughter an inflated census count of the number of Jewish households."

One night while driving the girls home, I also tried to explain to Gabby that, in our country, there are quite a few more Christians than Jews. I could sense her shock and disbelief at my words. Sure, she has many Christian friends. She's met many more at her public school. She also knows full well that my side of the family is Christian. However, Gabby has grown up going to the Jewish Community Center's (JCC) preschool, and she also goes to religious school at the temple. She just naturally assumed that, because so many of the people she's around are Jewish, most of the rest of the world would be Jewish too.

Our younger daughter Molly, sitting in the seat next to her sister and in the midst of the "why stage," repeatedly asked why there are more Christians than Jews. I didn't have a clear-cut answer as to why. But I did let my daughters know that they certainly were not alone. I explained to them that being Jewish was something to be proud of. Like most things in life, it doesn't matter how many other people are like you. What's important is how good you are at being who you are and how you feel about being what you are.

Since that conversation, Gabby and Molly have begun to accept that they are in a minority. However, there are times when I can see Gabby getting a little miffed at the lack of attention her religion receives in American culture. This past December, our family found ourselves in Boston's Quincy Market. As we walked with our cousins in and out of the stores and around the food stands, the atmosphere was festive. People laughed and scurried about, big shopping bags in hand. Pretty lights were strung up all over, wreaths hung on doors—some of the shops even had that fake frost painted in their window corners. It was the holiday season. It was the *Christmas* holiday season.

Suddenly, Gabby exclaimed in disgust, "Ughhh! Don't they know I'm Jewish?"

As we stifled a laugh, Bonnie replied, "No, honey, they don't." But then, more sympathetically, "I know. Sometimes it stinks when there are no Jewish decorations."

Later that night, after the kids were in bed, Bonnie and I discussed how hard it can be to comfort our daughters on this subject and, at the same time, teach them the realities of being in a minority group. It's not always easy, or fun, to be different.

Given the dominant Christian culture in our society, I can see that it would be easy for our girls to want to be a part of it. This is particularly true when many of their friends are not Jewish. When Gabby goes to play at one of her Christian friend's houses, the talk between the two sometimes falls into a comparative exchange.

"I'm getting an American Girl doll for Christmas."

"Well, I'm getting one for Chanukah."

"I get lots of presents on Christmas morning."

"Well I get presents for eight days."

Some things never change. I can remember having a similar conversation with one of my Jewish friends in first grade.

Gabby's Jewish friend Sarah has a Christian friend, also named Sarah. The two Sarahs are inseparable. From what her mother tells me, the two Sarahs' conversations during playdates get to be quite deep.

"How can you not believe in Jesus?"

"Are you going to heaven?"

They are naturally curious and open, trying to figure it all out. In the future, I expect to see a talk show entitled, "Religion Rap—with Your Hosts Sarah and Sarah." They need to get through first grade first though.

No matter how hard we try to surround Gabby and Molly with Jewish elements and protect them from being swallowed up by the dominant culture, we just can't isolate them. Going to a public school, they will always have plenty of Christian friends and be exposed to a variety of religions other than their own. Fortunately, the Ann Arbor public school system is sensitive to its diverse population. The teachers plan lessons that help the kids learn about many different cultures. In addition, there are no Christmas pageants in which all the kids are required to participate.

I always laugh at the story that my father-in-law tells of when he was in kindergarten, singing in the Christmas concert of his Providence, Rhode Island, elementary school. "You should have seen the look on my mother's face," he relates, "especially when the teacher announced to the audience that I was to sing a solo of "Silent Night." Her jaw hit the floor. The next year, I was in Hebrew day school."

One alternative for us would be to send our daughters to the Hebrew day school here in town. It is a fine school with a great reputation. There, our girls would get a solid Jewish education and be surrounded by other Jewish children. However, Bonnie and I feel that, in our case, Gabby and Molly are getting a strong foundation in Judaism through the programs at the Jewish Community Center and at the synagogue. Besides, the public schools in our community have fantastic teachers and curricula. Growing up in Ann Arbor myself, I always felt that I gained tremendously by being in a setting where I could make friends with kids from different backgrounds.

There's no way for us to shelter our children from the dominant Christian culture—especially since I am Christian. They get plenty of Christianity from my side of the family as it is. And they seem to be doing just fine. I think what makes the difference is that Bonnie and I have worked extra hard to instill a Jewish identity in them.

Perhaps, as an interfaith family, we have an advantage because we know we have to make a conscious effort. Yes, they learn a lot about my religion, but at the same time, we go to great lengths to teach them about Judaism. They know that even though their mother and I are of two different religions, they are not of both religions, and they seem comfortable with who they are. Rather than hiding from the reality of Christianity, we tackle it head on by answering their questions. This way, they have the self-confidence to handle themselves and feel good about being Jewish, while not panicking just because a Christmas carol comes on the radio.

Nowhere is this more of a test than when my wife and daughters accompany me to church. Although their visits with me there are infrequent, Bonnie has confided to me that she worries about all the talk of Jesus during the service. We wonder if it will confuse Gabby and Molly. We just continue to instill in them that I am the Christian and, though they are there to keep me company, it is not their service or their house of worship.

By attending the many JCC and synagogue functions as a family, the message is driven home that they are Jewish girls in a Jewish family. It is through these activities that I find so much joy in seeing their Jewish identity soar. This year, Gabby started her formal religious education at the temple—her first leg on the journey to becoming a bat mitzvah and taking on the responsibilities of a Jewish adult.

To be honest, when Bonnie and I discussed the religion that our children would have before we were married, I wasn't sure that I could raise Jewish children—especially if it meant going through this coming-of-age ceremony. Was it the fear of the unknown? Was it concern over what my role, as the Christian father, would be in the process? I had been to only one bat mitzvah. I can remember thinking, "How on earth will I know how to help my kids through this?" Was it fear of what my Christian family would think? They might say, "Hey, Jim, we put up with your raising your children Jewish, but now you need to tone it down."

Looking back on it today, I have no idea why I was so afraid. Now that Gabby has begun her religious education, I can't imagine why she *wouldn't* become a bat mitzvah. Knowing how much she enjoys going to religious school on Saturdays, she would probably be eternally upset with me if I told her that she couldn't mark this milestone. It would also be contrary to the plan that Bonnie and I have put forth to raise our children as Jews. If you're going to do something, you might as well do it right. I can't imagine feeling anything but a deep sense of pride the day she becomes a woman in the eyes of the Jewish community.

In the meantime, before I let her grow up too fast, I'd like to savor every moment of her burgeoning wonder at the world around her. I know that she's going to ask more and more questions. I can only imagine our future conversations about religion. "Daddy, tell me more about Christianity." Or, "Daddy, do we believe in the same God?" She surprised me once with her questions. The next time, I'll be ready and eager to answer her. I would tell her all that I know and all that she would like to hear. Although we are of different religions, we share the same God. The gap between our two faiths gets a lot narrower when I look at it from that perspective. I hope that she would find comfort in that thought, as well.

Postscript

A mother in an interfaith marriage reported that her daughter burst into tears one afternoon, saying, "But Mommy, I am good." It was November, and a Christian cousin had explained that she was trying hard to be good so that Santa Claus would come. Through the child's eyes, issues like being good for Santa Claus can be very confusing, even when parents have made a clear choice of religious identity for the child. Many families do not have direct conversations on the subject of what it means to be an interfaith family. Children may learn songs, hear stories, and make crafts and food related to

Jewish holidays at home and at the synagogue. At the same time, they may be exposed to other symbols, hear different songs, and experience other celebrations in the homes of grandparents and extended family members. Without specific conversations that help children make sense of the situation, the child cannot answer the question, Who am I?

Children want to know who they are and how their family and life work. It is important to let your children know that you welcome a conversation on being an interfaith family. This is true even when the question is one that you don't have an answer to or that triggers a feeling of discomfort for you. It's fine to say that you don't know the answer, as long as you make sure to resume the conversation at a later point, when you have had time to think about or research the answer. Your children will get better information from you than from their peers. Help them anticipate which holidays they will be celebrating and where they will celebrate them, while at the same time talking about which holidays they will be able to enjoy with their relatives on both sides. Tell them who they are in terms of their religious identity. Encourage them to come to you when they feel confused. Think of these conversations as giving children a road map to their unique family.

A. C.

11

Fun and Games at the Jewish Community Center

It didn't take long after Gabby was born for my wife to start thinking about where to send her for child care. To tell the truth, the thought caught me off guard. After all, "our baby" wasn't even a year old yet. I hadn't even considered that my little girl would have to spend time in some strange place without Bonnie or me to look after her.

Even though I was scared just thinking about it, I nonetheless wanted to help with the decision as to where our daughter would begin to socialize with other kids. Where she would get her first little bits of schooling. Where she would learn to share. Where she would eat her graham crackers. Where she would make new friends. And, of course, where she would have her feelings hurt when another kid stole her pink plastic horse. Where she would skin her knees on the playgr . . . All right, stop. That's enough. I was reading too much into it. But still, it was an important decision.

So, Bonnie and I started looking at the different child-care centers around town. Some we had heard great things about (you know, the ones with a three-year waiting list), and some we had heard a few unflattering remarks. Then there was the JCC and its Early Childhood Center. I was naturally a little concerned when Bonnie brought up the idea of enrolling our daughter there. Sure, it had a remarkable reputation. Still, I was a little apprehensive about sending Gabby to a place where, as I mistakenly thought, she would learn nothing but Hebrew. I wanted her to have a "normal" child-care experience.

"You will look into it with me, right?" Bonnie had asked.

"Honey, I don't know."

"Everyone says they have excellent teachers there."

"I know, but will she learn about stuff other than Israel?"

As it turned out, the JCC taught kids a lot about Israel and Judaism. They also taught myriad non-Jewish subjects. As we looked at it in depth, the JCC had everything we were searching for in a child-care center: great teachers, a wonderful director and staff, a spacious playground for sunny days, a big gymnasium for rainy days, fun classrooms where the children could play and learn, and best of all, a warm, welcoming atmosphere. The decision became easy. Gabby would begin her school career in the Bunny Room of the JCC's Early Childhood Center. Now I couldn't wait for her to start.

As time went on, my little girl became a big girl at the JCC. She was learning a lot. As it turned out, I was learning a lot, too. Year after year, we continued to register Gabby at the JCC. Why? Because it offered so much more than I could have ever imagined.

One of the biggest reasons was that it gave us a sense of community. The JCC was not just for kids. We parents were a welcomed part of the center, as well. My wife and I not only got a feeling of belonging, but also a chance to be involved. Bonnie began serving on the board of the JCC. It was a great opportunity to have a say in our children's education. I got to volunteer at various functions, including fund-raisers, Shabbat dinners, and other holiday functions, and I've been known to serve ice cream at Family Fun Night. They actually expected me to scoop more than I ate. Where else could you find this much trust?

This sense of community did not stop there, either. The seniors in our area were extremely active at the JCC; they also participated in many of the Early Childhood Center's holiday parties and events. After a while, we got to know many wonderful and intriguing people of all generations and backgrounds. There was a special bond that we shared, as we were all part of this center.

The JCC's special events provided our family with an opportunity to meet other families with whom we have a lot in common. Many were part of an interfaith family, just as we were. It was reassuring to have friends who faced similar issues. However, as alike as some of our backgrounds were, there were many families who came from all over the world. We found it just as fun to develop friendships with families from Russia, Japan, Sweden, Israel, India, and other reaches of the globe. Even while most families at the JCC were Jewish, the center welcomed people of all faiths. Friendly and enlightening—what more could we ask for?

These functions also provided a much-needed chance to celebrate Judaism with our community. It was fun to get on the phone and call up friends and ask, "Are you going to the Sukkot dinner tomorrow night?" And while we taught Gabby Judaism in the home, these functions reinforced her Jewish education by creating wonderful memories for her. In addition, during the day when she was in class, the teachers would read stories and create fun projects for whatever holiday was approaching. During Yom Kippur, for example, Gabby learned all about Jonah and the whale and painted a picture of Jonah inside the whale's stomach. Every Friday, the kids celebrated Shabbat with a song leader and baked challah to take home for dinner.

For Gabby, aspects of her Jewish culture and faith were now starting to click. In fact, one Friday afternoon as I picked Gabby up at school, she began singing, "Shabbat Shalom—Hey!" Later that evening, as Bonnie lit the candles, Gabby began reciting the blessing. Bonnie and I exchanged a surprised look. Sure, we had said it on many Friday evenings before, but now, with the JCC reinforcing it at school, she was actually learning the Sabbath prayers at age one and a half.

I was struck by how beautiful it was that Gabby had memorized these religious blessings. Then I thought, "This is it. She really is learning Judaism. Wow." Sure, we had given her a Hebrew name, but she didn't have to do anything for that. This was Gabby taking an active role in her religious education. Hearing her recite the blessings was like watching a seed that we had planted when we decided to raise her Jewish bloom into a flower.

Today, Gabby is a graduate of the JCC program and a bona fide first-grader. She continues to attend all the after-school functions with us and helps her three-year-old sister, Molly, with all the ins and outs of being a JCC preschooler.

As an interfaith family raising our children Jewish, we're never quite sure if we're sending a consistent message to our kids. Does my being Christian confuse them? I'm sure it does, to a point. But while I'll continue to be a Protestant and teach my children about my religion, I will always find ways to reinforce their Judaism. This is one area where we find the JCC to be of the most benefit. The center's Early Childhood Program provides that sense of Jewish culture, community, religion, and life that other schools cannot.

Postscript

Faced with the necessity of coming to a decision about your children's education makes all the theoretical discussions suddenly real. This moment of truth can be seen as an opportunity. It can be the beginning of creating family memories that will last a lifetime. It could be a good time for both parents to learn more about Judaism so as to be better teachers for their children, whether by taking a class, reading a book, or getting more involved with the synagogue. But it is also an important time to talk about what this moment of decision may trigger for you.

Some interfaith parents whose children attend Jewish preschools report feeling both delight at their children's love of school as well as a sense of being overwhelmed by all of the new words and holidays. Some also express the fear that they will become distanced from their own children or be left out of the family. These conflicting feelings can exist simultaneously and are not mutually exclusive. Nancy, a parent in an interfaith couples' group, whose child was about to start preschool at the JCC, asked, "When should I tell her that I am not Jewish?" The group responded supportively, suggesting to Nancy that she tell her now and not make it a family secret. They also advised Nancy to assure her daughter that the decision about her religious identity was the choice of both her parents and that together the three of them are creating a Jewish home, even as they figure out what that will mean for them. They also told Nancy not to hide her religious identity from her child's teachers.

Nancy's feeling of being left out could not have been anticipated until this couple enrolled their daughter in a Jewish school. It is important for the Jewish parent to be sensitive to the feelings of his or her partner. Most parents talk at length about their child's preschool experiences. It is important for parents to also talk about their feelings about being in a Jewish setting. It may be important for the Jewish parent to offer more support, perhaps to become more active in the child's education. Whatever the solution, the Jewish parent should always try to be a supportive listener. There may be moments in your family life that trigger unanticipated feelings. The challenge is recognizing these moments as opportunities for learning, growth, and increased family closeness.

A. C.

Part IV

CELEBRATING
THE HOLIDAYS

12

Teaching My Parents
about Judaism

"*Gimel!*" my dad shouted as he scooped up the pile of jelly beans in the center of the table. He was referring to the letter of the Hebrew alphabet on the dreidel that had just landed faceup telling him, "you win." It was Chanukah, and we had invited my parents over for our annual dinner and game of dreidel that we always play with such fervor. As I mentioned, in my family, we play for jelly beans in addition to the usual chocolate coins, called gelt.

We had just finished eating a wonderful meal of chicken, broccoli, and latkes (potato pancakes) with applesauce. Earlier, my parents had helped us light the menorah (the candelabrum of eight candles, plus one "helper" candle, that is lit during Chanukah). My mom and dad even sang some of the traditional songs with us. While they didn't do any of the cooking, they did play with our two daughters, Gabby and Molly, so we could prepare the meal.

In many Jewish homes, it is not unusual for the grandparents to help out with religious celebrations—unless, that is, they're not Jewish. By now, I've had about seventeen years to learn a lot about Judaism from Bonnie. My mom and dad, on the other hand, are relatively just starting out. They began getting serious about learning more when our first daughter, Gabby, was born. Before then, they had an interested, but limited knowledge of my wife's religion. The introduction of a grandchild into the family can have that effect. My parents are very loving and family-oriented. Fortunately for us, they were really excited about helping their grandchildren celebrate their holidays.

The first step that Bonnie and I took in bringing my parents into the fold was explaining what each holiday was about. For example, we told them what Shabbat is, why we eat apples and honey on Rosh HaShanah, and why Bonnie fasts on Yom Kippur. The first time I built a sukkah (hut for eating and sleeping in during the holiday of Sukkot), I explained to my dad why I just built this, in his words, "tool shed with a leaky roof." He was only trying to be funny. But, all kidding aside, my dad thought the whole tradition of inviting friends and family over for a special meal to be eaten under the stars was really "neat." It made me feel good that he took the time to ask about it and learn another aspect of the Jewish religion. Today, my parents know all about Sukkot and can speak intelligently about it to their grandchildren. I dare say, they know more about it than some of my Jewish friends who do not pay much attention to this holiday. I wouldn't call Mom and Dad experts, nevertheless they're knowledgeable. For instance, they probably couldn't tell a *lulav* from an *etrog* (two symbolic objects found in the sukkah), but at least they've seen them and know where they belong.

I think my parents enjoy learning as much as they can about their grandkids' religion. It helps them feel a lot more comfortable and welcome when they help our children celebrate their holidays. My mom and dad are just as much of a fixture at the Jewish Community Center preschool holiday functions as any other kid's grandparents. Granted, they often have to be reminded when a Jewish holiday is coming up (having holidays based on a lunar calendar doesn't help).

Of course, living in an interfaith family can have its advantages. It opens all sorts of windows to parts of society that you never knew existed. I know my life is richer for having met Bonnie and learned about Judaism. I try to pass these discoveries along to my parents, as well. I remember one day I was sitting around talking with my mom and dad about how lucky we were that all of our parents had been relatively accepting of our marriage. Many parents (of both religions) do not favor intermarriage. From a Jewish standpoint, one reason, I explained, is that many feel that it's harder to perpetuate their culture and religion if their members keep intermarrying. I don't think my mom and dad had ever looked at it that way.

Helping my parents understand their grandchildren's Judaism is not all about, "on this holiday you sing this, and on this holiday you eat that." Living in the United States, my parents and I have always been in the majority. For the first time, I was able to show them a perspective that I had learned from a minority culture. Now, in my own way, I have become a part of that minority. And, like it or not (and they do), my parents have, too.

Postscript

Holidays can be a particularly challenging time for families with different faith backgrounds. But holidays can also be a wonderful time to reach out to extended family of different faiths. Within the Jewish calendar year, each holiday has it own special message that offers a unique opportunity to educate both Jews and non-Jews about Judaism in a warm and welcoming way.

Since many Jewish holidays are observed in the home, family and friends of other faiths can be invited both to help prepare for and to participate in the celebration. Ever since Karen and David were married, David's Jewish mother, Aviva, has invited Karen's Protestant family to the Passover seder. After a few years of participating, Aviva began inviting both Karen and her mother to help prepare the meal. The informal time spent preparing food together gives all three women the chance to share stories of family holidays and imagine together what Passover might be like with grandchildren present. The families also come together for Shabbat dinner on special occasions, such as the Shabbat nearest Karen and David's anniversary. While Karen's father doesn't feel comfortable leading the prayer over the wine (Kiddush), *he shares his love and knowledge of fine wines by bringing new kosher wines to try at holiday celebrations.*

Opportunities for learning and teaching about other religions through holidays often go both ways in interfaith families. Karen observes Advent by lighting a colored candle on a special table wreath during each of the four weeks preceding Christmas. She explains the tradition as being similar to the concept of the Hebrew month of Elul, a time for Jews to begin preparing themselves mentally and spiritually for the High Holy Day season. Though the two holidays have quite different meanings, they share an emphasis on having a period of preparation, supporting a common belief in the need to approach religious observances with thought and intentionality. After some years of working out the kinks in this approach, Karen and David now celebrate holidays with both sides of their family in a way that is comfortable and fun for everyone.

J. W.

13

Shabbat:
The Holiday That Comes Every Week

It's 5:42 Friday evening. I'm in my car driving home from work, when all of a sudden I realize I've been singing for the last six minutes. I'm not singing to anything on the radio or CD player. No, I'm singing, "Shabbat Shalom—Hey!" It's not a song one expects to hear coming out of a Christian's mouth. So why am I singing this particular song?

Of all the Jewish holidays, I especially enjoy celebrating the most important one—Shabbat. This is the Jewish Sabbath, and it comes every Friday at sundown. After a week like the one I've just had, it's a welcome respite. Every single day we rushed to work, preschool, doctor appointments, a softball game, and a birthday party at Chuck E. Cheese's. Now, it's time to slow down and enjoy a nice dinner with the family. In the old days, my grandparents used to observe the Christian Sabbath on Sunday in a similar fashion. For them, it was a day to rest. Stores were closed; nobody rushed off to a hockey game. In addition, the dinner played a big role, in gathering the family to the table to say a prayer and be together. It's too bad that that practice is no longer as common as it used to be.

At 5:54, I pull my car into the garage. Dog-tired, I enter through the laundry room and BAM! I'm hit on both legs by my two little cuties, who have wrapped their arms around me while yelling, "Daddy's home!" Carrying the two of them, seated on both of my feet, I walk like Frankenstein into the kitchen to greet Bonnie. She's already set out the Shabbat candles and the *Kiddush* cup of wine on the table. The challah is just coming out of the oven. The house smells great. I feel a little bit like Fred Flintstone home from a day at the quarry—only Fred never had to help cook. For Shabbat dinner, we often grill. I'm pretty good at cooking with fire. Anytime there's an element of danger involved in food preparation, I'm there. It must be a tribal instinct.

It's 6:20 and the chicken is done (a little burned, but done). It sits on the platter, smoldering and waiting for us to dig into it. But first, we must say the blessings. According to Jewish law, we're supposed to wait until sundown. Unfortunately, sundown for us, in Michigan, is on the western edge of the eastern time zone. In the summer, we'd have to wait until after 9:00 P.M. Our girls go to bed at 8:30, so we start early.

The ritual begins with Gabby doling out yarmulkes to everyone, based on their favorite color. Then, Bonnie and Gabby light the candles and recite the blessing over the Sabbath lights. It's great to hear my daughter actually use Hebrew. Molly, who has big brown eyes that get even bigger with the candlelight, takes it all in.

After each blessing tonight, we make sure to say the prayer in English, as well. We feel strongly that the kids should know what the prayer means, instead of simply rattling off the Hebrew. Being Protestant, and not growing up around Hebrew, I also enjoy the translation. When I first learned the Hebrew blessings a few years back, I had no idea what they meant. Then, when I heard them in English, I realized that they were very similar in nature to the prayer my father recites at Christmas dinner. Saying the prayers in English makes our family ritual feel more inclusive and accessible for me.

Since our daughters were born, we've begun to say the blessing over the children—first in Hebrew, then in English. "May God make you as Sarah, Rebekah, Rachel, and Leah."

"Sarah who, Daddy?" Molly asks. "Gabby's friend, Sarah?" Bonnie and I exchange a humorous look and then proceed to tell her about the four Matriarchs of Jewish history.

I admit that I needed a little brushing up on that part of history, too. My parents never said this type of blessing over my siblings and me. So, before the first time we recited the prayer, Bonnie gave me an overview of who the four Matriarchs were. The fact that this is a new concept for me and that I'm asking my daughters to emulate Jewish women does not bother me. If I look in the Bible of my youth, I'd find these women. Besides, the four Matriarchs are not bad examples to follow.

Next, I say the blessing over the wine. We raise the antique *Kiddush* cup and drink from it. For the kids' benefit, it's filled with kosher grape juice. Bonnie holds the cup tightly for the girls when they drink, so that it's not dropped. After all, this cup belonged to her grandmother. Every time I drink out of it, I feel in awe of the tradition behind it. In my mind, I picture Bonnie's *bubba* as a young mother, and my father-in-law as a boy. I picture her also holding the cup firmly in her strong hands, preventing him from dropping it to the floor, preserving it for future generations. "Thanks, Bubba," I think to myself.

Finally, we say the *Motzi*, or blessing over the challah. It's about time, too. Molly, for the last ten minutes, has said nothing but "hallaaaah, hallaaaah, hallaaaah" over and over again. Of course, she's finished her piece before I've even said the word *Baruch*.

Some time after six (by this time, I'm too relaxed to remember what time it is) we sit down at the table and enjoy a good meal. I appreciate the fact that we're all sitting down to eat together now. I start to remember for the first time since last Friday that this is what Shabbat is all about—thanking God. We thank God for all that God has given us. We thank God for our health and the gift that we can share this moment on a nice, quiet Friday evening. Maybe the food's not perfect, but the time together certainly is.

"Strange isn't it?" I think to myself. When Bonnie and I were first married, she told me that she would like to have a nice Shabbat dinner now and then. And every once and a while, we did. Now that we have two daughters, we've been making every effort to see that they learn about Judaism and what it means to be Jewish. My mind starts counting the weeks backward a few months. Then it strikes me. Without realizing what we were doing, we had been observing Shabbat every Friday night as far back as I could remember. Not bad for a couple who originally wanted to just fit it in when we could. Never in my wildest dreams did I imagine that I'd look forward every week to a Shabbat dinner. After a crazy week, I am grateful for this moment to catch my breath, count my blessings, and spend time with my family.

Postscript

Parents who are not Jewish often wonder what role they can play in reinforcing the decision to raise the children within Judaism. Children need both of their parents to nurture and support a religious identity decision. Whereas the Jewish parent often serves as an ambassador into Jewish life and rituals, the role of the parent from another faith background is equally important.

Rick, a Christian dad, was at home alone with his two young children one Friday evening. His Jewish wife, Rachel, a nurse, unexpectedly had to work an extra shift. Rick realized that his kids would still expect to do their special shared Shabbat family rituals—the lighting of the candles, the grape juice, and the challah, for which Rachel always took the lead role. So Rick set out the challah and grape juice and hunted around, unsuccessfully, for the Shabbat candles and candlesticks. Unable to reach Rachel on the phone, he decided instead to use birthday candles for the Shabbat blessings and, not having any other candlesticks to use, inserted them into the challah and poured out a cup of grape juice for each child. He and the children joyously sang the Shabbat blessings together. Responding to the new twist of the birthday candles in the challah, each child made a wish and promptly blew out the candles.

When Rachel came home from work later that evening, she thanked Rick for maintaining the weekly ritual for their children in her absence. Rick told her how much he had enjoyed helping the kids have Shabbat. When he told her about the "new tradition" he had begun, she laughed and suggested that they add a "Shabbat wish" to the weekly moments of blessing. On future Friday nights, Rick and Rachel went back to using their Shabbat candles and candlesticks and let the candles glow until they burnt down, but they now incorporated the ritual of a "Shabbat wish" into the candlelighting ceremony. Rick felt great that he had added something original to their family's celebration of Shabbat.

With his children at his side, Rick was following through on his desire to be a part of, not apart from, his family's celebration of Jewish life. Shabbat offers weekly ritual time for shared family memories. The commitment of both parents to this shared family time instills a comforting, secure sense of religious identity for Jewish children. All families, especially interfaith families, can benefit from putting their family's personal touch into ritual celebration.

P. B.

14

The High Holy Days:
A Time for Both of Us to Learn

September, for many Christians in the United States, brings memories of "back to school," football games, and apple cider. These are the same feelings Bonnie experiences. However, September, to her, means something much more significant. It is time for the Jewish High Holy Days of Rosh HaShanah and Yom Kippur. This is a time to be with her family, go to services, dip apples in honey, and atone for sins of the past year.

Because of all that goes on at this time of year, both partners may be experiencing warm, fuzzy feelings during this month, but for different reasons. I certainly don't equate the start of the football season with the importance of the High Holy Days, but I do feel it is necessary for my wife to realize that her Protestant spouse did not grow up with the same experiences. Fortunately for me, Bonnie has always been understanding and eased me into the Jewish experience at a pace that was comfortable for me. Important note to the Christian partner reading this: Don't think for a minute that I'm going to sit here and tell you that your Jewish spouse has to do all the accommodating. You should consider putting down your caramel apple, turning off the game on the TV, and trying just as hard to understand the significance of the season for him or her.

The first time I experienced the High Holy Days with my wife, it wasn't until after we were engaged, and I wasn't sure what to think. We went to her dad's house for Rosh Hashanah. I loved being with all of her family. I also loved the tasty food that was served non-stop for two days. Going to temple, though, was a different story. It was my first time *ever* in a synagogue. It's not like going to a different church, where a few minor details are changed around but otherwise it's all basically the same. At my in-laws' temple, not only was it a foreign holiday for me, but there was a lot of Hebrew used in the service. I didn't know what was going on. The fact that I had to sit there for three hours did not help my restlessness. Most Protestant services are only one hour long, *and* they're in English. Despite the fact that Bonnie did her best to explain what was happening and what some of the Hebrew meant, and Bonnie's parents tried to make me feel as welcome as possible in their synagogue, I felt lost.

After temple, we went back to Bonnie's parents' house, where Bonnie helped me learn more about her holiday. She explained the meaning of the Torah portion read that day. We dipped apples in honey "for a sweet new year." Even though my wife was surrounded by friends and family, I was really happy that she spent extra time with me that day. The Christian partner can have feelings of being alone or isolated on Rosh HaShanah. A little hand-holding can go a long way.

Eight days after Rosh HaShanah is Yom Kippur. To a Christian, this can feel like a double whammy—first the Jewish New Year, and then the Day of Atonement. Rosh HaShanah is festive and happy, but Yom Kippur has a serious and somber aspect to it. Protestants don't have anything like this holiday. Catholics have confession, but not a whole day devoted to atoning, praying, and fasting.

We had talked about Yom Kippur in advance so that there would be no surprises. This kind of advance preparation is very important for interfaith couples. The fewer surprises, the better. I did not fast, but felt it was important for me to respect my wife's situation. (Note to Christians: Don't eat a big bowl of Cheerios in front of your spouse on this day. Try to do your eating discreetly and out of sight.) While Bonnie did not expect me to fast along with her, she was still unaccustomed to being around someone who was eating. (Note to Jews: Remember that your partner, if he is not fasting with you, will still need nourishment. Don't take it as a lack of respect if he eats. Just try to be someplace else if it makes your stomach growl like Godzilla with a bellyache.)

Once again, I went to services with Bonnie—actually, twice that day. Being at the temple was not my idea of fun. Where I really enjoyed myself was watching and admiring my wife during this most holy day for her. I was not about to complain. This was my wife's day, and I would see her through it. To my great surprise, she slipped me a protein bar during the service and told me to go take a break outside. I was floored. I was speechless. About the only thing I could do was give her a peck on the cheek and head for the door. When I came back ten minutes later, she had a big smile on her face. I think it was caused by a combination of giving me pleasure and knowing that it would soon be time to break the fast.

At first, I didn't think my wife could fast all day. Bonnie loves food, so I didn't know how seriously she would take the fasting. I was sure she wouldn't make it. In the end I learned a lot that day. I developed a newfound respect for her and her religious convictions. Not only did she make it, she did so without a single complaint.

Yom Kippur can feel like a long holiday, but they reward you with a big spread of food at the end. The most significant thing we learned was that it is important to be respectful of each other's feelings on this day. Bonnie's thoughtfulness and validation of my attempt to support her on this important day had a positive impact on my overall experience. Giving each other the support to make it through strengthened our relationship that much more.

In short, when it comes to the High Holy Days, Jewish partners can help by remembering that their Christian partners may have feelings of insecurity or of not fitting in with your family or temple. Sometimes, they might just be plain ignorant of your traditions, feelings, and experiences. Don't forget to help guide them. It'll pay off in the long run.

Each couple needs to decide whether they will accompany each other to their respective houses of worship. This of course gets more complicated when children arrive. In our case, Bonnie and I decided that I would go with the girls and her to temple on their holidays, and they would travel with me to church on mine. We feel this is extremely helpful in learning about each other's religions—especially when it comes to teaching our children. Just as important, it is a show of support and love for each other. As a couple, we constantly work to show our spouse that his or her faith is important. As parents, we also need to send the right message. Just because Daddy is Christian, it doesn't mean that he doesn't care about his family's Jewish faith. That's why he comes to temple with us. Along the same lines, Mommy and the children can show Daddy that they care by going to church with him on special occasions.

Bonnie and I have been cautious when it comes to taking the kids to my church. At an early age, we could see how it might get confusing for them. To prevent that, we made sure to have them accompany me only once in a while—Christmas Eve being the most notable service. We also emphasized the point that they are Jewish and were there only to help me with my celebration. This is Daddy's church; they go to a synagogue.

Today, I am a fixture at the temple with my family. When the kids come along with me to church, they enjoy the special event. Bonnie and I have set a pattern that is predictable for our children. They have been well versed in our game plan and know what to expect. Consistency is the key. Over time, thanks to Bonnie's help, I've found myself feeling more and more comfortable with her holidays. I have learned the rituals of the different services. I have made friends at the temple. I have even learned some Hebrew. Every year

I see how much more I can follow along in the prayer book by improving my recognition of the Hebrew letters and words. I now look forward to Rosh Hashanah and Yom Kippur. I actually get a warm, fuzzy feeling over these holidays. After all these years of marriage, it's getting to be that September can't roll around without me breaking out my football, fall clothes, and shofar.

Postscript

While making the decision to be a Jewish family means a great deal of adjustment for the partner of another faith, it also means more adjustment and accommodation on the part of the Jewish partner than most ever consider before the fact. The High Holy Days are a time when that reality comes into especially sharp focus, as you encounter the mood of the season and the challenges in sharing unfamiliar worship and other rituals.

Rosh HaShanah is challenging enough, but Yom Kippur is on an entirely different level. Unlike Rosh HaShanah, when there was only a morning service and the rest of the day was spent with family, Dana was used to spending the whole day in synagogue on Yom Kippur. Before they had children, Jack, a Methodist, would treat the day like almost any other, including going to work when it fell on a weekday. Dana felt abandoned and alone on what she considered one of the most important days of the year, but never said anything, as she did not want to impose her observance on Jack. When their oldest child reached preschool age, Dana asked Jack to stay home from work so that she could spend the day in synagogue and not have to leave their child with babysitters on a day that should be spent differently. Jack readily agreed, and as the kids got older and attended the synagogue's children's programs, he began to attend the morning services with Dana. He had, in fact, been willing to do so all along, but since Dana never raised the matter, Jack saw no reason to do so.

Dana was surprised at how much it mattered to her that her partner was, on some level, sharing the solemnity of the day, even if it was not his own holiday. Jack's desire to be a caring and supportive partner made all the difference. And it turned out that the themes of the day resonated with Jack in a meaning-

ful, even profound way. He appreciated the fact that though the day is, in so many ways, God centered, its goals are humanistic, inspiring worshipers to grow and become more than they had been. Jack appreciated that the images of God were accessible, if somewhat different than he was accustomed to finding at a prayer service. The notion of t'shuvah—repentance and return— was not only familiar, but was, for Jack, an essential religious teaching. The approach was new, but echoed values that he had held closely throughout his life. He was intrigued by the notion of responsibility for resolving one's relationships with others as grounded in the relationship with God, and he appreciated the opportunity for self-reflection that Yom Kippur provided. While Jack chose not to fast and attended only the morning service on Yom Kippur, the day became one of important spiritual growth for both Dana and Jack, as well as a valuable shared experience.

H. J.

15

Sukkot?
Never Heard of It

I have to admit I never knew that a holiday called Sukkot existed until I met Bonnie. I'd be surprised if 10 percent of the non-Jewish population of our hometown of Ann Arbor had heard of it either. It's not a holiday that gets a lot of press. This is really a shame, because, over the last decade, I have found it to be one of the most enjoyable holidays of either religion. It is a time to remember the Jews who wandered the desert for forty years, a time to celebrate the harvest, a time to be grateful for all our blessings, and a time to spend with family and friends.

The year 1999 was a big one for my family. Not only was our second daughter born, but we also moved into a new house. Coincidentally, we happened to move in right before Sukkot. After getting the majority of boxes emptied and put away, I came across our disassembled sukkah. A sukkah is a temporary structure that Jewish families erect in their yards during Sukkot to remind them of the portable huts the Jews lived in while they were wandering in the desert. Usually they are built of wood, though prefab sukkot made of metal piping are becoming popular, and they are decorated with all sorts of items, including gourds, cornstalks, and paper chains.

No Sukkot celebration is complete without a *lulav* and *etrog*. The *lulav* is made up of three branches that are placed together in a holder—one of palm, one of willow, and one of myrtle. An *etrog* is a citron, which is a fruit, like a big aromatic lemon. (Ironically, the only other time I've ever heard of a citron was when my Aunt Alice baked some into her delicious Christmas bread that she sends us every December.) After reciting a special Sukkot blessing, each person takes a turn holding the *lulav* and *etrog* together, shaking them in each direction. Because the *lulav* and *etrog* are made of real plants, you need to order fresh sets each year from your synagogue.

We had bought this particular sukkah kit (lumber, brackets, screws, and all) at a temple fundraiser a few years ago. As I took inventory of the different pieces, I was delighted that it was almost time to put it up. This meant, for the time being, that I wouldn't have to find a place to store it in our already overstuffed garage.

When the first day of Sukkot arrived, I dragged all the parts to the backyard. It only took me an hour and ten minutes to raise the structure. Over the years, I have gotten this process down to a science. I'm like an Indy pit crew with my power drill. Sometimes my father-in-law is in town to help me (although he just holds the bag of screws). Then we can build it in under an hour. You should see the sparks fly—we're good!

I was just putting the finishing touches on our sukkah when my next-door neighbor stopped over to talk. He had a wary look on his face. He was curious about this "shed" that I was building that took up a majority of our small backyard. He was greatly relieved when I told him about my wife's holiday and that the sukkah would be coming down at the end of Sukkot. Once I told him about the festival, he didn't care how long it was up. He thought it was nice to have something different going on in the neighborhood.

One of my favorite things about Sukkot is that it is a time to celebrate with neighbors, friends, and family. It is a tradition to invite guests to join in a holiday meal in the sukkah. Bonnie and I put a table and chairs in the sukkah, invite our friends over, and have meals in it. It takes backyard barbecuing to a whole new level. When our friends come over, we cook tasty dishes, the kids and their friends make decorations, and once the kids are in bed, the grown-ups sit in the sukkah for hours talking. It's refreshing to be with company in a different environment, where the TV is off and the phone is left in the house. You'd be amazed at what this does for the quality of conversation.

Another great part of Sukkot is the requirement that the roof of the sukkah be covered with branches, palms, or leaves, so that a certain percentage of the sky is visible. It must be open enough so you can see the stars at night. I've always loved to camp, and now that Gabby and Molly are into camping, I think this might be the year we pull out the sleeping bags. Sure, we're not in the woods or mountains—it's just our backyard. However, there's something rewarding in being able to teach my daughters about their holidays. To have fun while doing it is a bonus. We can pretend we're in the desert with Moses. The stars will be out (hopefully), we can sing songs, and in the morning, when my back is stiff, I can take a long hot shower.

Our lives can get pretty routine at times. Why not take the opportunity to do something different and build a sukkah? If ever there were a chance to do the out-of-the-ordinary, a chance to turn your backyard into a magical place, this would be it.

Sukkot is a fun holiday. I'm very lucky to be able to take advantage of this time with my wife and kids. When Daddy starts building the sukkah, it's like an electrical charge hits Gabby and Molly. Many of our Jewish friends do not build a sukkah because it wasn't a part of their childhood experiences. When they come over for dinner in our sukkah, they laugh at how it took a Protestant to get them to celebrate the holiday in the proper way. I'm proud that I can help my kids know that this week of Sukkot is special. This week, our family will be doing things differently around the house. This week, they will learn a little more about their Jewish heritage.

Postscript

For one interfaith couple, Hannah and Mark, Sukkot is their children's favorite holiday. The weekend before Sukkot begins, uncles and cousins from both sides of the family come together to build the sukkah. Since Sukkot comes at the beginning of the school year, the family creates an informal invitation that is given to every student and teacher in the children's class, as well as other friends, family, and neighbors. For Hannah and Mark, Sukkot is a wonderful opportunity to get to know new people and renew old friendships. Anyone and everyone is welcome to an open-house afternoon of socializing and enjoying the bounty of the fall harvest foods such as nuts, apple cider, popcorn, and garden vegetables. Guests are also invited to bring something to help decorate the sukkah, such as gourds, flowers and herbs, popcorn strings, or peppers.

Sukkot is also known as the "Season of Our Joy" and as such is often compared to a Jewish Thanksgiving. At the end of their Sukkot open-house afternoon, Hannah, Mark and their children lead their guests in the holiday blessings, and then each mentions something for which they are thankful. Hannah notes that she always takes the opportunity to welcome everyone and offer thanks for friends and family, who bring richness and diversity to their lives. At the end of the day, the family hosts a potluck meal in the sukkah, including homemade soup and bread prepared by Hannah, her mother, and Mark's sister. The beautifully adorned sukkah remains throughout the week, and each child has the opportunity to invite one special friend and his or her family to a more intimate dinner in the sukkah on another evening of the festival. In this way, the family has created a Sukkot celebration that is welcoming and comfortable for all of their friends and relatives. The celebration of Sukkot has become, for this family, a way to bridge differences and be inclusive.

J. W.

16

Will Santa Bring Me Presents
Even if I'm Jewish?

Ahhh, yes. The December dilemma. It's something we parents in interfaith families look forward to all year. The confusion. The doubt. The inconsistency. It doesn't have to be this way, though. There are workable solutions. With a little effort and perseverance, you can get through the season with your family and sanity still intact.

My wife and I have striven hard for an answer that fits our particular situation. In the above paragraph, I mentioned "workable solutions." The emphasis here is on the plurality of the word "solutions." Every family will have unique issues to face. There is no single correct way to resolve this dilemma.

However you decide to handle it, the earlier you begin working on how your family will deal with the Christmas and Chanukah season, the better. Bonnie and I started while we were engaged. We suddenly realized that yes, one day we would have children. What to do? We had no clue. We just knew that it was better to go into family life with a game plan. We felt that if we waited to figure it out after our children were born, we would be susceptible to disaster.

When Bonnie and I decided that we were going to raise our children as Jews, it clearly meant that we were not going to raise our kids in both religions. At the same time, we knew that whatever plan we came up with would have to be flexible. At that time, we hadn't had children yet, so we couldn't possibly know what it would be like when they were born and the reality hit us. We had to create a plan that allowed for minor adjustments. It would have to be like the Constitution of the United States—the door should always be open for change under the right circumstances. The important thing was to make sure we were consistent and that the kids knew they were Jewish and therefore celebrated Chanukah.

Having already decided to raise the kids Jewish, we knew they would celebrate Chanukah, and I would *help* them celebrate their holiday. That was the relatively easy part. But I am Christian and still celebrate Christmas. Christmas is an important holiday for me, and I wanted our children to learn about my holidays. In addition, Christmas was a time to be with my parents and my siblings, both of whom are married and have children. We are a close family and all live in the same town. We always get together for the holidays. How would my children react if they had to sit still and watch their cousins open a bunch of presents from Santa? And it's not just the presents. The spirit of the holiday is everywhere during the Christmas season. There are trees to be decorated, cookies to bake, and lights to be strung. Santa's jolly pink face is everywhere—even on your can of Coke. These are all fun things that I grew up with and was not about to give up, even if American marketing would let me. So we decided that Bonnie and the kids would *help* me celebrate my holidays. They would wind up learning about Christmas and what Christmas means to me. But as Jews, they would understand that they were only assisting Daddy with *his* celebration.

In 1996, Gabby was born. Three and a half years later, Molly came into our world. It was easy when Gabby was an infant—she didn't ask questions. All we had to do was stick to our plan. But by the time Molly was born, Gabby had started to ask *lots* of questions.

"Who in our family is Jewish? Which grandparents are Christian?" She was starting to categorize things. It's cool, she does this with her stuffed animals: "These three are bears, these two are froggies," and so on. A completely age-appropriate activity.

But then she started to ask, "Does Daddy celebrate Chanukah? Do I get Chanukah *and* Christmas presents? Will Santa bring me presents, even if I'm Jewish?"

We had been afraid something like this would happen. Gabby started putting two and two together in an appropriate three-year-old way, and realized that it's the Christians—not the Jews—who celebrate this holiday with the tree and Santa. Well, this led to one big anxiety attack that she wasn't going to get *any* presents. We calmed her fears by reminding her of all the nice Chanukah presents that she was going to get. We also explained that it's much more important to give than to receive and that both holidays are about giving.

We didn't want to put too much emphasis on the gift aspect. As our daughters have gotten older, we've been able to explain to them that the holidays are not centered on presents, but rather are to celebrate special events that took place a long time ago. We have made sure to tell the story of Chanukah. The girls know all about Judah Maccabee and the miracle of the oil that burned for eight days. In addition, in religious school they have learned about the importance of religious freedom that the Chanukah story relates.

Likewise, we have not shied away from teaching Gabby and Molly about why my side of the family and I celebrate Christmas. We want them to know that it isn't because of Santa Claus; it is about the birth of Jesus. They understand the story, and that my Christian beliefs are not theirs. As a result, their assisting me (and their subsequent interest) has chiefly been focused on the secular American traditions of Christmas. Bonnie and I still go to great pains to make sure they know that even the nonreligious aspects of my holiday are not a part of their faith. But I do enjoy their help.

Once we were sure that they understood the ground rules, we didn't want our kids to focus on the differences in our family. Instead, Bonnie and I have tried to nurture a sense of identity for our children that they could be proud of, while realizing that their religion and culture are just part of who they are. This, we believe, is the most important part. They are a lot of things: they are girls, they have brown eyes, Gabby likes to dance, Molly likes to laugh at the dog, and, yes, they are Jewish. Daddy is tall, he has green eyes, and he is Christian. Mommy is pretty, she likes chocolate, and she is Jewish.

The next obstacle we had to overcome was keeping a consistent approach to the holidays. At first, my Protestant parents kept asking us what kind of gift, if any, to give the girls on Christmas morning. Christmas or Chanukah presents? We had to admit, we were slightly unprepared for the question. The gifts had never had an identifying label attached to them. But then again, the girls had never asked—until now. This is why we had made our plan flexible. We knew we'd have to adapt to the unexpected.

After we discussed it for a few days, we finally decided how we'd explain things to our kids. Chanukah was simple; the kids get Chanukah presents. Christmas, which we celebrate at my parents' house, was more complicated. We decided to tell Gabby and Molly, "Santa brings you a couple of late Chanukah presents on Christmas, because he knows you're Jewish." What we've now worked out is that my parents and in-laws give the major gifts to our daughters on Chanukah. Meanwhile, my parents save one or two smaller Chanukah presents for Christmas morning. This seems to work well for us. The message to the girls that they are Jewish is consistently reinforced, but they're not excluded from the activities during my holiday. It's also important that my parents, who love to give presents, are not denied their pleasure on Christmas morning either.

We explained it to the girls using the birthday party analogy. It's not *your* birthday that's being celebrated. You're there to help the birthday girl celebrate *her* birthday. But it doesn't mean you're not allowed to have fun, too. And when their grandparents give them a little something on Christmas morning, it's like getting a goody bag at a birthday party, a treat for helping to celebrate that day.

While working through this not-so-simple problem, both Bonnie and I realized we were uncomfortable with other solutions and ways to phrase things to our children. Early on, Bonnie felt that it just wasn't right to celebrate Christmas at all with the kids. However, I wanted to share with the girls some of the joy and special feelings that I had from my childhood. There were emotions that we both felt that the other one couldn't possibly know. We had to make some tough decisions. Yes, there is a tree in our house, but it is *my* tree. Bonnie and the girls only *help* me decorate it. We do everything we can to keep it in a different room from the Chanukah decorations. Of course, the separation is much easier on the years that the two holidays don't fall during the same week. My wife and daughters also attend church with me on Christmas Eve. We join up with my parents, siblings, and all the little cousins. This is another way for Bonnie and the girls to *help* me celebrate my holiday.

At first, we made a conscious effort to separate the two holidays as much as possible and identify who celebrated what. As time went on, though, handling the holidays has become more second nature to us. However, there's always that lingering thought in the backs of our minds, "Are we confusing our children?" Fortunately, Bonnie's stepmother offered us a refreshing bit of wisdom. She said, "One day out of the year isn't going to make or break their Jewish identity. It's how you raise your kids as Jews the other 364 days that counts."

In the end, we knew we were creating an interfaith family and would have to approach the holidays from a different angle than same-faith marriages. We are both comfortable with what we've decided. It may not work for everyone, but it fits our family nicely. In the years to come, I'm sure we'll have to face more surprises and twists. However, we have a solid foundation on which to build. We'll be ready.

Postscript

Jeff and Suzanne knew that the magic of Santa Claus was very important to Suzanne's Methodist parents, who wanted to pass along their many family Christmas traditions to all their grandchildren, including three-year-old grandson Sam, who was being raised within Judaism. Suzanne's mom was especially concerned that Sam might "spoil the magic" for his other young cousins if Sam did not believe that Santa delivered everyone's holiday presents.

Jeff and Suzanne created a strategy in which they told Sam that he would receive most of his presents during his holiday, Chanukah, but that Santa knew Sam was Jewish and would include a Chanukah present for him when Santa brought Christmas presents to Grandma's house for his Christian cousins. They shared their strategy with Suzanne's parents, who agreed to cooperate. Neither Suzanne nor Jeff saw the need to discuss it with Jeff's parents.

"Santa will be bringing me Chanukah presents this year!" three-year-old Sam announced to his somewhat surprised Jewish grandmother as she tucked him into bed.

Afterward, she asked Jeff and Suzanne about the comment, wondering how she should have responded. Jeff and Suzanne then shared their "Christmas strategy" with Jeff's parents. Jeff's parents were able to see the bigger picture of their young grandson's Jewish identity and managed not to "freak out" at the mention of Santa. Jeff's mom acknowledged that Sam clearly knew he was Jewish and felt joy in the Jewish rituals Suzanne and Jeff created in their home. Suzanne shared that her parents try to reinforce their grandson's Jewish identity as they are able, but are very grateful that Sam is a part of some of her family's traditions as well. Jeff's parents understood that Suzanne's parents needed a way to share their holiday traditions with Sam.

Jeff and Suzanne now share their strategies on a range of issues with both sets of grandparents, and it has helped tremendously. Not every situation will turn out as ideal as this one did for Jeff and Suzanne. But the only way your parents can support your decisions is if you tell them what you need them to do to be supportive.

P. B.

17

Eggs and Plagues:
Easter/Passover Issues

Spring in Michigan is always a welcome sight—just ask anyone who has ever spent a winter here. So when the snow melts, and the crocuses bloom, everyone tends to get a little giddy. "Whadaya mean I can't wear shorts? It's fifty-two degrees. It's hot out!" Yes, people are excited. Of course, in my interfaith family, we have an extra reason to be elated. It's the season for Easter and Passover.

My wife and I each have fond memories of our holidays. For Bonnie, it's *matzah brei* (eggs and unleavened bread fried up in a pan) and getting together with her cousins for Passover. For me, it's Easter eggs and Disney World for spring break with my family. To this day, just the smell of vinegar (used in the dye) reminds me of the brightly colored eggs that the Easter Bunny hid for us. Like Christmas and Chanukah, Easter and Passover can also evoke strong emotions in interfaith families.

Instead of letting these feelings be a source of strife for us, we decided to make them a springboard for embarking on a whole new set of experiences. We did not want to deny one of us our traditions by trying to pick which holiday would be celebrated in our household. As with our December dilemma, Bonnie and I decided that we would each *help* the other celebrate his or her holiday. We do this for other holidays. In that respect, Easter and Passover are no different.

One of the most important aspects of these two holidays, for both of us, is being with our families. My wife must be with her family for Passover, or it just isn't the same. The big gathering of her parents, aunt, uncle, and cousins (and now their kids) is an annual happy occasion—even if it reaches the decibel level of a 747. We all get together in Boston for at least one of the two seders (Passover meals). We learn about Moses and the Pharaoh, the Ten Plagues, and the significance of the Passover food. There's lots of singing and lots to eat. (The food is delicious, but too much matzah gives me lead-belly.)

For my family on Easter, it is also important to be together. As kids, my brother, sister, and I used to dye Easter eggs on Saturday night. The morning of Easter Sunday, we'd wake up and scurry around the house looking for hidden eggs to put in our Easter baskets. As we grew older, we started to spend our spring break vacation in Disney World. Because this break always occurred over Good Friday and Easter, it became a tradition to enjoy our holiday with Mickey. Today, my whole family, nuclear and extended, makes the trip to Florida. Like my wife and her side of the family, it just wouldn't feel right spending the holiday any other way.

There are many customs associated with these two holidays. However, the religious aspects of Easter and Passover are not to be ignored. Bonnie usually accompanies me to the Easter church service. I once asked her if all the talk of Jesus made her feel uncomfortable. She replied that, as foreign as it was, she still viewed it as an educational experience. She said that going to church with me gave her an opportunity to learn more about my faith and background. Because we're on the road for Easter, I never quite know what to expect in a different congregation from my hometown. I'm always afraid that the minister will say something that might offend my wife. I don't know exactly what that would be; yet I still worry. Fortunately, my fears have not even remotely come true.

As Bonnie learns from my Easter experience, I, too, enjoy taking in the Passover scene. My first seder with her was on the campus of the University of Michigan, while we were just dating. We went to a house with a bunch of friends, where our host proclaimed that putting on this seder made for a lot of happy mothers back home. Because we were students, we did a lot more eating and talking than anything. We skipped over quite a bit of the Haggadah, the book containing the prayers, songs, and story of Passover. I was not intimidated in this setting, but I worried how would it be when I experienced my first Passover with her big family in a "real" seder?

My wife has a wonderful family, but I was nervous about fitting in and not sticking out like a sore thumb at the dinner table. True to form, though, they went out of their way to make sure I *didn't* feel uncomfortable. I was assigned duties around the kitchen just like everyone else. I can proudly say that I helped grate the horseradish for the Passover plate. (Each food on the plate is symbolic in some way. Horseradish symbolizes the bitterness of slavery the Jews experienced in Egypt.) However, I did feel out of place when passages were read in Hebrew or, even worse, sung in Hebrew! Not knowing the language is bad enough, let alone not knowing the tune. What was reassuring for me was feeling that everyone there *wanted* me to be a part of the family.

The first couple of years spending Passover with Bonnie's family were a huge learning experience for me. There's a part of the seder when the leader of the service breaks a piece of matzah called the *afikoman*. In some families, the kids hide the *afikoman* and hold it for ransom. In Bonnie's family, sometimes the leader will hide it in the room and make the kids hunt for it. Now this I could relate to!

Over the years, I've gotten to know the different prayers, songs, and symbolisms of Passover. I've found that I can make the holiday as easy or as difficult as I want it to be. I've chosen to make it an experience from which I can absorb a lot about my wife's religion.

As we learn more about each other's holidays, we, as parents, are better prepared to impart to our children the meaning of Daddy's Easter and the traditions of their own Passover.

Postscript

On the surface, the close timing of Passover and Easter may seem easier to navigate than the December dilemma. While Easter is at least as important theologically, if not more so, to Christians than is Christmas, for some families it is less important as a time to gather together. Passover, on the other hand, is the most family-oriented holiday for Jews and holds a place of much greater importance for many than does Chanukah. Passover commemorates the Exodus from Egypt, an event that is accepted by Christians as part of the common Judeo-Christian history. For this reason, a Christian partner in an interfaith relationship may not experience the theological conflicts about Passover that most Jews feel about Christmas. The themes of freedom that are expressed during a Passover seder can be widely appreciated by partners of other faiths.

Since Passover is a home-based holiday, it is as much about the individual family as it is about theology, ritual, and history. Jewish partners need to realize that while for them a seder may conjure up wonderful family memories, it can be an especially strange and daunting experience for someone who has no prior experience with this ritualized meal. Not only are there unfamiliar foods, songs, rituals, and often a fair amount of Hebrew, but each family's seder also has its own quality and tone. In many families, a seder may be raucous, argumentative, or even silly, which can come as a surprise to someone who might expect a ritual meal to be serious and staid. A Jewish partner needs to be sure to prepare his or her partner not only about the history of the seder meal, but about the rituals specific to their family.

At the same time, Christian partners need to be prepared for the fact that their Jewish spouse may have uneasy or even negative associations with Easter. While the exterior symbols of Easter, such as baskets of candy and elaborate brunches, are appealing, the real theological underpinning of the holiday, resurrection, may be uncomfortable for Jewish partners. An addi-

tional level of discomfort may come from the Jewish partner's awareness that the celebration of Easter, with its accompanying Passion plays, has historically been a time when Jews were the most persecuted.

As in other situations regarding religious rituals, interfaith couples should communicate with each other about anxieties and expectations; they should be prepared to share with each other what is important and personally meaningful about each of their holidays, to what extent they would enjoy and appreciate their partner's participation, and in what areas they feel the least comfortable. When children are part of the picture, it is important to convey to them which holidays are important to which members of the families. Offer clear explanations about why they celebrate the holidays that they do. Teach them the difference between these holidays and the holidays that they may help other relatives celebrate.

R. G.

Part V

MEETING
MY OWN NEEDS

18

If I Can't Play Santa Claus, at least I Can Be the Tooth Fairy: What I Need for Myself as the Christian Member of the Family

When Gabby was five, she lost her first tooth. Actually, it was her first two teeth. They were getting crowded out by two newly erupted adult teeth and needed to be pulled. The dentist was having a two-for-one sale, so we yanked them.

After the tears were dried and the Popsicles slurped, I suddenly and delightedly realized, "Hey, the tooth fairy's got to come tonight." (What's the going rate these days anyway?) I had to be ready. So I explained to Gabby how the whole thing works. "You put your teeth into this little box and put it under your pillow. While you're sleeping, the tooth fairy will come into your room and exchange the teeth for money."

Together, Gabby and I put the teeth into the special silver box my mother gave her. We delicately hid it under her pillow as I tucked her in. Later that night, while she slept, I tiptoed into the room, searched for the box, finally found it underneath her Pooh Bear, took the teeth out, put the cash in, and crept out the door, banging my ankle on the dollhouse and nearly ruining the whole effort. As I closed the door and stood there in the hallway with Bonnie, a big grin came over my face.

"You know," I said, "this is a major milestone for us, as parents. It's our first time playing tooth fairy. It's just like playing Santa Claus—all the make-believe and sneaking around at night."

Then, as soon as it had come, my smile went away. "Oh, wait a minute. I don't get to play Santa Claus," I thought sadly. I observe the Christmas holiday, not Chanukah. My wife and daughters celebrate Chanukah, not Christmas. So I don't get to be Santa Claus.

After experiencing the fun of being the tooth fairy (no, I didn't dress up in a tutu), it dawned on me that, for the last five years, I had been denied the opportunity to play Santa for my kids. They don't celebrate Christmas, so I've always given them Chanukah presents during the eight days of the holiday. There really isn't a "Chanukah Harry" to dress up as, so the thrill of delivering presents in the middle of the night has been missing since my children were born.

However, the arrangement in our family, I reminded myself, works. I wouldn't want to change a thing—especially not just so I can fill stockings at midnight. Upon further reflection, I felt pretty happy about the course Bonnie and I had set for our family. Fortunately, I could now get my stealthy magical-character fix from playing the role of the tooth fairy.

As the only Christian in our family, I've come to realize that I have certain needs, too. It's always a tricky line to walk in making sure that I fulfill those needs and not undermine what my wife and I have worked so hard to achieve for our family. I could be really demanding and insist that we all celebrate Christmas and Easter exactly as I did as a kid, but where would that get me? I suppose it'd get me a one-way ticket to resentmentville.

Raising a family, just like the marriage itself, is full of compromises. I care deeply that my wife and daughters' needs are met. I make sure that I deliver a consistent message about their Jewish identity. I enjoy helping Bonnie teach them about Judaism—both the culture and the religion. At the same time, I also feel that it is important to meet a few needs of my own. After all, it works both ways. I don't want to be the one building up resentment, year after year.

I do have my short list of things about being Christian that are important to me. Bonnie knows how sincere I am in nurturing a Jewish household, and she, in return, makes sure to take care of my needs. During Christmas, I have a tree—right there in the family room. I know some people have difficulty working such a strong symbol into their family dynamics. However, it works well in our situation. Everyone in our house knows that this is Daddy's tree. Bonnie and the girls help me decorate it, but they know they are Jewish and Chanukah is their holiday. They do not celebrate both. Because of this arrangement, I feel less uptight about teaching my daughters a few things about my religion and culture. Having the Christmas tree in our home brings back a lot of happy childhood memories. Not having it would be a mistake. Being an interfaith family doesn't mean we have to sterilize the house of one of our religions. The last thing in the world I want to feel is that I can't celebrate my own holidays.

While the Christmas tree is often one of the biggest hot-button issues of interfaith families, to me, it is not the most important. First of all, it matters more to my family what we do the other 364 days of the year in teaching our daughters about being Jewish. Second, it matters more to me that I work on being a good Christian every day of the year. For instance, I enjoy accompanying Bonnie and the girls to temple. In addition, on Sundays and the Christian holidays, I like to go to my church. It's part of being Protestant. Occasionally, and especially on Christmas, I like for my wife and daughters to come with me. This is not because I want them to listen to the sermon and hopefully convert. I just like the company. There's nothing better than having your family around when something is important to you.

Fortunately for me, I have that support from my family. I know this is the biggest gift of all that they can give me. As the only non-Jew in the family, I sometimes wonder if I'll feel lonely, out of place, or even sheepish about observing my own religion. Because Bonnie and I try so hard to accommodate each other's needs when going about our daily lives, I've managed to feel fulfilled.

At 6:00 the morning after the tooth fairy visited, Gabby came running into our bedroom, jumped on top of us, and yelled, "The tooth fairy came! The tooth fairy came!" As she threw her pint-sized bear hug around my neck, I was reminded once more that, yes, my most important needs were being met.

Postscript

When needs are met in a relationship, they often lessen in intensity; when needs remain unmet, they continue to carry significance (and possible resentment!). Understanding and meeting your partner's needs is important every day of the year, but for interfaith couples, this sensitivity to some of the complex family memories that the holidays can engender is especially important. Sometimes, a partner in an interfaith relationship may experience a feeling of "aloneness" as holidays approach. The best antidote for this feeling may be talking to your partner about what you need for yourself and why you need it.

When Laurie, who is Catholic, was engaged to Martin, a Conservative Jew, she was feeling sad and lonely as the December holidays approached. She told her fiancée, "This Christmas I need a really big Christmas tree." Fortunately, before Martin reacted, he asked her what this really big tree meant to her. Laurie's memory of the really big tree was connected to her childhood memories of happy holidays before her parents divorced. Listening to her explain her needs enabled Martin to understand the meaning of the tree for Laurie—even though he might have wanted to say, "No way." That year, Martin found Laurie the biggest blue spruce that could fit into a small apartment. She was very grateful and viewed the tree as Martin's way of acknowledging her needs.

Every year, Martin still asks Laurie if she needs her big tree because he knows that the Christmas tree holds such significant childhood memories for the person he loves. Since Laurie knows that Martin is willing to fulfill her needs, the needs are no longer so pressing for her. Surrounded by her husband and children, she celebrates Christmas with her sister's family and her mom, helping them to decorate a very large blue spruce. Laurie's need for a close and united family has been met by the enduring love she has received from Martin.

P. B.

19

Keeping the Faith:
Why I Have Chosen to
Maintain My Christian Identity

What a relief. I had just finished doing a reading at Barnes and Noble Booksellers and had breezed through a relatively easy question-and-answer period. Everything was over, and I was putting my coat on when a good friend of mine came up and asked me what was easily the most difficult question of the day: "How do you feel being the only Christian in your Jewish family?"

I told her to wait for my next reading and submit her questions in writing one week in advance to give me time to prepare. Seeing that she wasn't going to let me off the hook that easily, I had to stop and think of a way to express my feelings accurately. After all, this was a potential minefield of emotions for anyone in an interfaith family. Further, she wanted to know how I felt about my children not believing in Jesus as the Son of God.

She wasn't trying to be rude—and I certainly didn't take it that way. I'd known her for quite a while. I knew that she was a devout Christian and one who liked to take part in spirited conversations about religion. She was not a person who judged others based on their beliefs. She was just genuinely curious.

I told her that honestly sometimes it was hard on me. There had been times when I'd wondered if I'd made the right choice. If I believed in my faith so much, how could I allow my own children not to believe in it? Would it be better if I converted to Judaism? Before the kids were born, I thought that there was a chance that I would feel like a black sheep in my own family.

However, when Bonnie and I were married, we decided to focus on the similarities of our religions. We knew that Judaism and Christianity had some fundamental differences, but there was so much more that the two had in common—especially the morals and values that they both taught. We felt that there was a way to make this work, without either one of us having to give up our faith.

In addition, we decided that we would raise our children in a way that celebrated their Judaism, but also let them know that being Jewish was just a part of who they were. By helping our girls to understand it this way, we had demonstrated that sometimes family members had different faiths—just as they also had different physical and personality characteristics—and that was OK.

I told my friend that since our daughters were born, I had yet to feel like an outsider in my own home. My six-year-old knew full well that we had different religions. However, it really had been enjoyable for me to help her learn about Judaism. At the same time, it had been a lot of fun watching her make an effort to include me. Last year, when we were lighting the first candle for Chanukah, everyone yelled, "Happy Chanukah!" While the hootin' and hollerin' was going on, she reached over to me, pulled me down to her level and whispered in my ear, "Merry Christmas, Dad." For a "daddy-daughter moment," you just couldn't get any better than that.

As far as my own children not believing that Jesus was the Messiah, well, I had never been one to say which religion in this world was the correct one. While my faith has always been strong, my daughters and I still loved the same God, and that was good enough for me. The important factor here was that Bonnie and I were raising them in a faith that had wonderful traditions and taught excellent values. The last thing we wanted was for them to grow up without any religion at all.

My friend seemed satisfied with my answers, and we gathered up our kids and headed for the parking lot. She wasn't looking for a justification of why I had chosen the way I had. Rather, she was merely asking about something that was completely foreign to her. She and her husband were not only both Protestant, they were also of the same exact denomination.

I don't know if she felt that my choices were something that would have ever worked for her if she were in my shoes. I wouldn't expect them to. I have never been foolish enough to believe that everyone would agree with me on this issue. It is a tough one, and people handle it in different ways.

In fact, people often ask me why I have not converted to Judaism as one way to address the issue of our mixed-religion family. When Bonnie and I were dating and trying to figure out how we would make our interfaith marriage work, I looked at every option. It did not take me long, however, to know that I would not convert. Conversion would have been convenient, because it would have meant that my wife, kids, and I could all practice the same religion. But convenience is not why people should convert. It has to feel truly right. I don't feel that I can leave my religion. Is letting my parents down a factor? Oh, sure. Ultimately, however, both my parents and I know that it would be my decision to make.

I am a Protestant. I grew up this way, and my faith is as strong as ever. It's who I am. But it's not all I am. The Keen family mostly traces its roots back to, among other places, Clan Gunn of the Highlands of Scotland. I like to celebrate my ancestral background, even if it's more for fun than anything else. I believe that every American has a heritage and should be proud of it. That's what makes our country great. It's what unifies us—we're all from some-place else. I love teaching my girls about the places where their ancestors were born. I think it's wonderful that they learn about these people from Scotland, England, Ireland, the Comanche

Nation, Lithuania, Russia, and Poland. What a crew. And now, I am proud to say, there are some Keens who happen to be Jewish. I love it.

Though I am firmly rooted in my Protestant background, I do not, however, feel that conversion is the wrong choice for other people. You can still be proud of your heritage and adopt a new religion and culture. I have friends who have converted to Judaism. I think that they've made the right decision for their family. They are doing very well, and I am happy for them. They contribute positively to the Jewish community and are very involved in teaching their children about Judaism. I believe that their path was no easier than mine. While it works for them, it just wouldn't be right for me.

In short, I feel that I am the luckiest guy on earth. I have kept my religion while also having had the opportunity to learn about another great religion and culture. I get to have my cake and eat it, too. I'm a Christian who is fortunate enough to help raise a Jewish family. In my eyes, it's the best of both worlds.

Postscript

Unlike a couple who shares the same religious background, an interfaith couple cannot take for granted what holidays they will celebrate as a family or how they will celebrate them. Sonya, who is Episcopalian, and Henry, who is Jewish, made the decision to raise their children as Jews. Sonya was comfortable with the decision they made for their family. Her parents had belonged to an active church community, and she knew how important religious community could be for children. She enjoyed the traditions and practices of Judaism and the way that it was structured to bring the family together. Then one day, when her oldest child was five and beginning to ask questions about God and religion, he asked why, if she was Episcopalian, she never went to church. After all, he and his father and brother were all Jewish, and they went to synagogue. How could she really be Episcopalian if she never went to church?

After Sonya caught her breath, she realized that she felt she had been feeling inauthentic for a long time. It wasn't that she felt like she was faking being Jewish. She was very clear with her children that they were Jews, and that they were a Jewish family, even though Mommy was Episcopalian. But she realized that she no longer felt authentically religious or spiritual. Here she was, teaching her children to believe in God and to go synagogue on Shabbat to pray, but she wasn't living out those same things herself. That night, Sonya and Henry had a long and challenging conversation. Sonya voiced her need to be part of a church prayer experience and to attend church as regularly as possible. At first Henry was very uncomfortable with what Sonya had to say. He was worried that Sonya regretted her decision to raise their children as Jews and might not want to be involved in the synagogue anymore. Sonya reassured him that that wasn't the case at all, but that she needed to both fulfill her own religious needs and serve as an authentic religious role model, albeit not a Jewish one, for their children. After they talked some more, they both felt that they would be able to work out a way for Sonya to meet her own needs while still sticking to the decisions they had made about their family life.

If you are the parent whose religion is not being followed by the family, there will undoubtedly be times when you feel a sense of loss and sadness. Having a partner (and hopefully religious community) who recognizes and honors your gifts will help to balance that. It will also help to look for appropriate ways to incorporate rituals and traditions from your family of origin into your family life. There may be ways to transform some of the traditions that you grew up with into appropriate expressions of your children's religion. Be up front with your partner and yourself about your needs—both emotional and spiritual. Share stories about the traditions you grew up with, and encourage your parents to feel comfortable telling their stories to your children as well. As long as attempts are not being made to sabotage the decision that was made about the child's religious identity, the sharing of these stories can only create greater understanding and closeness in a family. Your nuclear family will create your own particular rituals and traditions, and those will become special and meaningful. Many involved in interfaith relationships find that their own spirituality grows as a result of having to spend time giving so much thought to what they will teach their children.

R. G.

20

Seeing the World
through Jewish Eyes

Helping to raise a Jewish family has exposed me to a whole new culture. You can even call it an American subculture. Learning about Judaism, its religion and way of life, has opened my mind to a lot of new perspectives. I look at current events differently. I use more Yiddish words than ever before. I now see and understand things in a new way.

I think that one of the best parts about helping to raise a Jewish family is that I understand a lot more jokes now. I've learned so much about Jewish culture that I get subtle bits of humor that I never used to. Jewish humor is actually a big part of American culture. Just look at how many Jewish comedians, writers, and actors there are: Jerry Seinfeld, Larry David, Eugene Levy, Rita Rudner, Billy Crystal, and many more. These talented artists write material that's funny to every American. But, they will often mix in a few Jewish elements that can only be understood by people familiar with Jewish culture.

I can honestly say that a lot of the humor went right over my head before I met Bonnie. Most of the time, I wasn't even aware that there was humor I was missing. Before Bonnie, one of my favorite comedians was Billy Crystal. When he was on "Saturday Night Live," he would do a skit called the "Joe Franklin Show." It was always "brought to you by matzah by Streit's. For the unleavened experience of a lifetime." I would sit there and wonder, "What on earth is he talking about?" I kind of knew what matzah was. It was a cracker thingy.

It wasn't until Bonnie invited me to one of my first Passover seders that I finally understood. During this holiday, Jews should not eat foods that are leavened (made with yeast). They eat special "kosher for Passover" foods. Matzah is the staple diet during this time. You eat these wafers by themselves, sometimes with butter or jam, sometimes with eggs and cottage cheese. Kosher food companies sell cakes and other treats made with matzah meal. They even make a cereal that looks (but doesn't taste) like Cheerios. Matzah is not made with yeast and, therefore, is kosher for Passover. Well, what should I see there in the kitchen during Passover? Right next to the bottle of Manischewitz kosher blackberry wine, sat—get this—a box of Streit's matzah. I just about flipped. It was an actual company. Suddenly, years of repeating that slogan, "For the unleavened experience of a lifetime," finally made sense. It *was* funny after all.

Getting to know Bonnie was the beginning of my Jewish humor education. My edification didn't come all at once, though. It took time. During our first year of dating, we rented Woody Allen's *Annie Hall*. Midway through it, I couldn't take it anymore. I didn't understand any of it. Meanwhile, Bonnie sat on the couch, just howling with laughter. She tried to explain what was so hilarious, but there was just too much Jewish shtick (look it up) for me to comprehend so quickly. Fifteen years later, I got up the courage to rent it again. This time, I finished watching the whole movie. It was a lot funnier than I remembered it. Woody's neuroses made a lot more sense after years of listening to the humorous stories and jokes that Bonnie's family had told me.

One of the funny things about Jewish humor is that once you understand it and people know that you'll find it funny, they tell you a lot more jokes. Bonnie's stepdad even includes me on his e-mail joke list. Here's one he sent recently (skip it if you've heard it before):

A guy named Goldstein gets marooned on a desert island. First thing he does is build a hut to live in. A few months go by, and he makes the hut a little bigger by adding on a bedroom and dining room. After a few more months, it looks like he could be there a while, so he builds himself a synagogue. A year later he decides to build a second synagogue.

Finally, after four years of living all alone on the island, a ship comes by. He signals it with a fire on the beach. The ship sees him and sends a rescue party. The crew lands on the beach, and the captain steps off.

Goldstein gives him a big hug. "Thank you for saving me."

The captain, seeing the buildings that Goldstein has erected, exclaims, "Wow! You've really been busy here. Did you build all this?"

"Yes, I did."

"What's that building there?"

"That's my house, complete with bedroom and dining room."

"What's that structure there?"

"That's my temple where I worship."

"What's that building next to it?"

"Oh, that's another synagogue."

"You worship at both this temple and the one next to it?"

"What, that temple? I wouldn't set foot in that temple!"

I told this joke to some non-Jewish friends and family. Guess what. It bombed. What I'm finding even funnier than the joke itself are the various reactions to the subtlety of the humor. Don't feel bad if you don't get it either. In time, you might. It's not a reflection of intelligence; it's a reflection of familiarity with a culture, a people's ability to make fun of itself.

In addition, the more time you spend around a certain group, the more you start using the group's language. Think about high school.

You and your friends had a few phrases and words that anyone outside of your peer group would have had a difficult time understanding. And by the time the old folks caught on to your lingo, you'd moved on to new words. I've been out of high school long enough to look foolish saying "da bomb." In fact, by the time I learned that that was a cool thing to say, the kids had already moved on to "tight" or something else they wouldn't tell me.

Medical professionals also have their own linguistic references. Doctors and nurses are always talking about EKGs and taking "meds" and giving shots "sub Q." After being around the doctor's office long enough, you start to understand what they mean. You even start talking like them. "Honey, I'm running down to the pharmacy to pick up my 'script.'" But, admit it. When you first heard these words and expressions, you were clueless as to what they meant.

That's exactly how I was in the Jewish world. Only now, I was learning words and phrases of real languages—Hebrew and Yiddish. It was bad enough that Bonnie was a law student while we were engaged. I had quite a time when we were around her classmates, trying to keep up with all the talk about "Con Law," "Torts," and "Civ Pro." Now, on every visit to her parents' home, it seemed that I learned a new word or expression.

I was also surprised to find that I had been using some Yiddish and Hebrew words for years before I met Bonnie—words like *shmuck*. This, by the way, is not as nice a word as I had thought. I found out that a common phrase, "the whole megillah," which I had used plenty of times in the past, actually comes from the word for "scroll," and refers to the reading of the whole story of the holiday of Purim, from the Scroll of Esther.

It wasn't long until I started using more Yiddish and Hebrew in my everyday speech. After a workout at the gym, I'd say, "That was a good *shvitz* [sweat]." After my daughters were born, I started saying things like, "Don't bump your *keppe* [head]." Or, pinching their chubby cheeks, I'd comment, "What a *punim* [face]." Even right now, I'm getting a little *verklempt* (choked up) thinking about how fast those kids are growing up. When you hear it enough around you, you get comfortable with it and start using it yourself.

Sometimes I feel a certain sense of "being in the know" using these phrases. When we go to Michigan football games, we usually sit in the same section, with the same people who've sat there for years around us. At one game last year, a guy and his son, who sit down the row from us, had to leave at halftime. When asked by the group why they were leaving early, the father replied that they were going to the son's bar mitzvah (why they were at the game at all that day, I'll never know—true-blue fans, I guess).

"Congratulations!" everyone told them as they sidestepped their way down the row to the aisle. "*Mazal tov!*" I automatically said when they finally got to me. The smile and thanks they gave me were not really any different than those that they gave to everyone else. However, the subtlety of my choice of words brought a hint of a knowing look in their eyes.

Using the Hebrew phrase for "congratulations" gave me a certain sense of belonging to another group. Although I am not Jewish, I can now identify with the culture. Yes, the humor makes more sense now, but so do more serious things related to Judaism, like the Holocaust. While listening to the news, any mention of current events in Israel causes my ears to perk up. It's all so much more relevant to me now, because it is relevant to *my* family.

I am not Jewish, but my nuclear family is. I'm proud of my wife and daughters. They include me in their culture and religion—and I *feel* included. After all, I help teach it to Gabby and Molly. That is very important to me. Not having that sense of inclusion was a big fear of mine before Bonnie and I got married. Today, not only am I a part of my wife and daughters' group, but I also have the ability to think and feel it. I still enjoy belonging to my Scottish-American, Protestant group, but it's a warm feeling being able to see the world through Jewish eyes, as well.

Postscript

One arena in which the feeling of inclusion or exclusion comes to the fore has to do with attending services at synagogue. When Marion accompanied her Jewish partner to Shabbat services for the first time, she felt like a stranger in a foreign land. Everything was confusing; she didn't know the customs, the language, little things like when to stand or sit, and even which way to open the prayer book. Hebrew was a foreign alphabet that she couldn't follow along. People wished her well in Hebrew or Yiddish, and all she did was keep smiling, because she had no idea what they were saying. She was grateful that her partner Rob was there to translate and explain.

Encountering the sounds and unique customs of a synagogue service may seem alienating. If you have never experienced synagogue services or Jewish holiday celebrations before, it may be helpful to anticipate your feelings ahead of time. Try to approach the experience with an open mind, and expect to feel out of your element for a while.

Marion's partner was able to orient her and translate for her throughout the experience. In addition, many synagogues publish a booklet that will explain their ritual customs to visitors. If you don't see such a booklet upon entering a sanctuary, take a moment to ask the usher if something like that exists. If you don't get the jokes, ask your "guide" to explain them to you afterward.

Learning about any new language and culture takes some patience and experience. Don't expect to feel at home in a synagogue on the first, second, or even third visit, to understand everything about the seder, or to get all the family's sense of humor. Give yourself a chance to experience and observe, and remember that the only way to begin to feel more comfortable is to learn through asking questions.

M. P.

21

Cut to the Chase —
Do You Feel Connected
to Your Family?

I have already mentioned that deciding in which religion to raise our kids was our most difficult decision. I was nervous that I would not feel connected to them if they were raised Jewish. I had no idea if they would relate to me or see me as part of the family if I were of a different religion. I wasn't sure that I'd know how to raise them in another faith. To tell the truth, though, I think that I would have been uncertain of what to do even if I'd married a Christian. There is no operating manual that doctors give you when your child is born. Yet now that I'm actually a dad, I realize that most of my fears were off base.

Don't take that the wrong way. I'm not belittling the feelings of anyone who might be in that situation. Those are very real anxieties that should legitimately be addressed. However, now that I've been through a significant number of years helping Bonnie raise our children, I see that I connect with them in so many other ways that I can't help but feel that I'm an integral part of their lives.

I help coach Gabby's soccer team—a cute bunch of ball-kickin', dandelion-pickin' girls, called the Ladybugs. I take Molly to gymnastics every Saturday morning, where I watch her bounce and tumble her way around the gym. The girls and I go to the museum together, where we can stare in awe at the dinosaurs. We visit the planetarium to see a show about the stars in the sky. We collect interesting rocks and try to identify them. We dig up brachiopod fossils near my office and take them to that same museum to have them identified. (Incidentally, we were very pleased to learn that a brachiopod was a mollusk-type creature that lived about 450 million years ago when Michigan was covered by a sea.) Each one of these activities is something that my daughters associate with me. They are fun things that we do together and continue to talk about at the dinner table. Gabby and Molly look forward to their next exploration with Daddy.

However, connecting to my children isn't just about taking them places. I'm the guy they expect to sing them a song at night, while I gently tickle their arms in a vain attempt to get them to fall asleep. Though Bonnie and I both read them stories, I'm the guy they expect to change the words around and make up new stories. Their mama may be the one who's best at kissing their boo-boos when they get hurt, but I'm the one who was roughhousing with them in the family room. Funny thing is, they always come back for more.

I am not at all an outsider in my family. I don't know why I couldn't see it before we got married. But until you've actually experienced life as a parent, you have no way of knowing how well you'll connect with your children, or in what ways.

What's become even more surprising for me, however, is the way that I'm also able to relate to my wife and children on a Jewish level. In the first year of our marriage, Bonnie and I took an "Introduction to Judaism" class. I wanted to learn more about what I had gotten myself into. She went along for a "refresher course" and to support me. We had always said that raising our family would be a joint effort, so taking the class together felt like the right thing to do.

Taking this class was one of the best things I have done. Learning about Judaism has helped me to become more comfortable with Bonnie's religion, culture, and family traditions. It has also given me a strong knowledge base from which I now am able to assist in teaching my daughters about their faith. So far, I haven't gotten a comment like, "What do you know about Moses, Dad? You're not Jewish." Gabby and Molly now associate me with so much of their religious education that I don't think I ever will hear anything like that.

Joining the Reform synagogue here in town has also been beneficial to our family. Do I feel like an outsider in the synagogue? No way. I may be the guy who drives the kids to the museum, but I'm also the one who takes them to religious school on Saturdays. The rabbi, Robert Levy, has been more than welcoming to our interfaith family. He encourages me to participate in the services in any way that I feel comfortable. During one of my first children's services, he even made sure that I got a chance to see the Torah up close. In the past, I had only viewed it from afar. Unexpectedly, it was a very heartfelt moment for me. It was pure acceptance of who I was. I was welcomed for just being me.

Where some congregations may be losing members, our synagogue is overflowing. Rabbi Levy's philosophy is to be as inclusive as possible. "Often, there is a mind-set in the Jewish world that it's all about numbers," he says. "How many people can we count as Jews? Instead, we should be focusing on the people as human beings and reaching out to them. When you lower the barriers to entry, everybody wins." The whole synagogue staff shares this philosophy, from the cantor to the director of religious education—all wonderful people who expect me to be as involved with my daughters' experience as much as any other parent.

In addition, knowing that there are other families in our situation in the congregation has enhanced my sense of belonging. When we go to temple, I'm surrounded by friends who are in the same interfaith situation that we are. It's comforting to know that you're not the only one out there who's trying to make a go of this. We have many friends who provide a great support group for us. It's more than helpful to bounce ideas off of each other and share hilarious stories about how our kids perceive their mixed-faith world.

Our friends Teresa and Barry, one such interfaith couple, told us how they like to go to a certain place for brunch on Sundays. It's normally very crowded, but if you get there early enough, you can beat the rush of people who show up after they get out of church. One Sunday, while racing to get there early, their five-year-old, Claire, shouted out from the back of the minivan, "Hurry up before the Christians get there!"

The fact that we get together with many of these intermarried families socially outside the temple makes it all the more enjoyable when we see them at temple functions. We try to attend as many of the family activities there as possible. They're a lot of fun, and our kids get to see *both* of their parents, as well as friends, participating in their religious activities.

Through the temple, I've gotten to know Rabbi Levy more and more. He is always glad to see us there. Just as important, he is always welcoming to me, the Christian parent—not the outsider. He is also a good friend to see at the temple, where I know that I belong and have a role.

I've learned that you can feel as included or excluded as you want. It depends on the amount of effort you put into being there for your family and wanting to feel connected. It has been important for me to make the effort to connect and be involved, and it has paid off. It hasn't been without complications, but we have been able to create a cohesive interfaith family. Over the years, I've found that my daughters don't need to put forth a conscious effort to include me or acknowledge the religious differences between myself and them. This past Christmas season, I would wake up every day to a fresh pile of Christmas cards that Gabby and Molly had drawn for me with construction paper and crayons.

They know my religion is different from theirs. But I am their dad and an integral part of their lives. I am important for the fatherly love that I can give them by playing dress-up in the family room or discovering how bubbles work at the science museum. I am also important to their religious identity. This is no clearer to me than when I arrive home from work on Friday evenings and am greeted at the door by two little girls who are as excited as birds around a feeder. "Daddy's home!" they shout. "Now we can have Shabbat!"

Do I feel connected? You bet!

Postscript

Connection in a family happens in many ways, and those areas of connection change and deepen over time. Special rituals, beloved foods, inside jokes, and memories all contribute to the deep tapestry of relationship that binds each family member to one another. In an interfaith family, spiritual connection is absolutely possible for every member of the family.

As in any relationship, the key to connecting spiritually in an interfaith context is openness, respect, and a willingness to learn. Taking a class on Judaism can help you together consider how you would spiritually parent your Jewish family. Likewise, the Jewish partner should also increase his or her awareness about the partner's religion and views on parenting.

Through learning and shared experience the playing field is leveled. When that happens, spiritual common ground becomes clear. Though the great religions of the world have differing theology and ritual, many universal values are shared. Some of these are a belief in a loving God, the centrality of family life, respect for learning, and a deep commitment to social justice.

Choosing to raise your children in one faith tradition does not mean that the responsibility for spiritual education becomes the sole domain of one parent. The responsibility for the spiritual life of a family must be shared. Taking the time to identify similar core values and learning to speak each other's religious language can enable you to begin a conversation about the spiritual life of your family, enabling you and your partner to parent as a team.

M. P.

Conclusion

If you've ever wondered whether you were doing the right thing, you often didn't fully discover the answer until you dove right in. Before Bonnie and I were married, I wondered, "Will I regret my decision? What if it doesn't work? Will I be isolated?" These were all questions that I asked myself over and over. I think most brides and grooms have these feelings, even without the intermarriage issue.

Despite the uncertainty, there was this little voice inside reminding me that I loved Bonnie. Would God really want me to lose my chance at spending the rest of my life with this wonderful person, just because our backgrounds were different? No. I decided that diving in was the only course of action.

I have no regrets. Our marriage and family dynamics haven't been perfect. Nothing in life is. However, our love is strong, and so is our desire to work things out. Even after our wedding day, I'd occasionally wonder how our children would turn out or if we should change how we approach certain holidays. We are committed to being flexible and to keep trying. I don't think that there's any issue we can't conquer.

Although there is a high rate of divorce in interfaith marriages, I believe that different-religion couples often have an advantage over same-religion couples. They're so used to communicating and solving their religious issues that they're ready when other problems inevitably hit the relationship. They've already established their model for working things out. This is, of course, easier when done before the wedding. However, it's never too late to start. Hopefully more interfaith couples will realize this advantage and discover that their differences, though complicated, can truly be a gift.

A reporter once asked me what I thought was the most unfortunate aspect of interfaith relationships. I replied that it is sad to see two people end their relationship with each other because they can't get past their differences in religion. I had just written an article for InterfaithFamily.com about how my family handles the December dilemma. A couple of days after its publication, I received an e-mail from a woman who had read my article. The day before, she had broken up with her boyfriend, because they didn't think that they could possibly resolve their interfaith issues. They had been going out for a number of years and were trying to figure out how they could live with each other and raise children. She was Christian, and he was Jewish.

After reading through several articles on InterfaithFamily.com, she realized that she and her boyfriend had made a mistake. She didn't yet know what the right answer was for her particular situation, but she was now inspired to find out. If other people could be successful at intermarriage, so could they. She told me that she was going to call her boyfriend and give it another try.

I think she was glad just to know that there were many other people out there in the same quandary. Few people go looking for someone of the other faith to marry. Many people even oppose interfaith relationships altogether. That's fine. However, whether you're all for intermarrying or dead-set against it, you can't escape the fact that people voluntarily and involuntarily fall into these relationships. Fortunately, there are ways to help them create a path to having a happy and feasible future together.

As I've said before, the experiences that I've related in this book are just one family's way of trying to make sense of this mixed-up world in which we live. I have many friends in successful interfaith relationships who have come up with different solutions. My hope in writing this book has been to share what has worked for us. If you learn nothing else from this book, please understand that there is a workable solution to just about any interfaith relationship. If two people love each other, and they have the desire to find the right formula and be honest with each other about their individual expectations and needs, they can succeed. Like a Yom Kippur congregation in the break-fast buffet line, there shouldn't be any stopping them.

Glossary

Note: I recognize that there are almost as many pronunciations and spellings of the following words as there are Jews. I have put them down here as my wife, my in-laws, and my Jewish extended family have taught me (unwittingly or not).

afikoman (ah-fee-KO-man): A piece of matzah that is hidden during the Passover seder, often for ransom by the parents or children, depending on individual family traditions.

baruch (bah-RUKH): The first word in many Jewish prayers. It means "blessed."

bat mitzvah/bar mitzvah (BAHT MITS-vah): The ceremony where a Jewish child comes of age, usually at age thirteen. Translated literally, it means "daughter/son of the commandment," or to put it another way, the age at which one is expected to take personal responsibility for responding to commandments. To be technically correct, one would not say, "I'm having a bat mitzvah," but, "I'm becoming a bat mitzvah."

bris (BRISS): Yiddish for the circumcision ceremony. In Hebrew, *b'rit milah*.

b'rit bat (BRIT BAHT): The ceremony to welcome the birth of a girl. Also called by its English term, "baby naming."

b'rit milah (BRIT mee-LAH): The circumcision ceremony (removal of the foreskin of the penis). In Yiddish, "bris."

bubba or **bubbe** (BUH-buh or BUH-bee): Yiddish word for "grandmother." *Bubbe* is actually the more common of the two.

challah (KHAH-lah): The bread eaten at almost every Jewish ceremony or holiday. Sometimes its shape is braided; sometimes its shape is swirled. Though some use the expression "challah bread," it is actually redundant.

Chanukah (KHAN-u-kah): The holiday celebrating the victory of the Maccabees over the Syrians. It is often called the Festival of Lights, referring to the lighting of the eight candles of the menorah. This symbolizes the miracle of the oil that burned for eight days in the Second Temple in Jerusalem after the Syrians were overthrown. It is actually a relatively minor Jewish holiday and is not the "Jewish Christmas," as many non-Jews believe. Literally, Chanukah means "dedication."

chuppah (KHUH-pah): The canopy under which the bride and groom stand in a Jewish wedding, meant to represent the home they are creating together.

dreidel (DRAY-duhl): The four-sided top spun during Chanukah. A game is played with dreidels for gelt or other candy. Each side of the top has a Hebrew letter for which players give or receive candy: *nun* = you get no candy from the pot; *hei* = you get half of the pot; *shin* = you cough up candy for the pot; *gimel* (everyone's favorite) = you win the whole pot.

El Malei Rachamim (EL mah-LAY rah-khah-MEEM): The prayer said at Jewish funerals, either at the end of the service in the synagogue, or at the gravesite. It asks God to take the soul of the deceased. Literally it means, "God, full of compassion."

etrog (EHT-rogue): The fruit used during the celebration of Sukkot. It resembles a big lemon and is always paired with the *lulav*. The English word for this fruit is "citron." Ironically, about the only other time one sees this fruit is at Christmas, when it is used in breads and fruitcakes.

freilach (FRAY-lakh): Yiddish word for "happy." This term most often refers to a traditional dance of Eastern European origin. Like the hora, it is very popular at weddings.

gefilte fish (guh-FILL-teh FISH): Yiddish term for traditional Jewish food of ground-up fish balls. The fish used is usually carp, whitefish, or pike, or a combination of them.

gelt (GELT): Yiddish for "money." Also refers to the chocolate coins wrapped in gold foil that are a Chanukah mainstay. Gelt is often used for prizes when playing dreidel.

Godforbid (gahd-fuh-BID): A slurring of the words "God forbid." It is often heard in the middle of a sentence, as in, "If anything should happen to you, Godforbid, at least you'll be wearing clean underwear."

goy (GOY); pl., ***goyim*** (GOY-eem): Someone who is not a Jew. Sometimes its usage is considered derogatory. The literal meaning of the word is "nation" or "people."

Haggadah (hah-GAH-dah): The book of prayers and songs that tells the story of Passover. Typically, everyone at the Passover seder has a copy of the Haggadah and follows along with the service.

hespeid (HES-payd): The tribute to the deceased at a funeral, much like a Christian eulogy. It is designed to summarize the accomplishments of the deceased and give comfort to the grieving.

hora (HORA): The traditional Jewish dance often seen at weddings and bar and bat mitzvah celebrations. "Hava Nagilah" is often the song played for this dance.

Kaddish (KAH-dish): Literally means "sanctification." Although there are many forms of this prayer, it is mostly known as the mourner's prayer. The majority of the words are in Aramaic, not Hebrew. It is recited not only at funerals, but also during daily services and on Shabbat.

keppe (KEH-pea): Yiddish for "head."

kibitz (KIB-its): The Yiddish word for nonproductive chitchat or goofing around.

Kiddush (KID-ish): The blessing over the wine. Sanctification.

k'riah (keh-REE-ah): The act of cutting one's clothing, either actually or symbolically, to represent the tearing apart that the death has caused in a mourner's life.

kugel (COO-gull): Yiddish term for a pudding or baked casserole type of dish. One common type of kugel is made with noodles and eggs. Another favorite is a potato kugel.

latkes (LOT-kahs): The potato pancakes eaten during Chanukah. They are fried in oil, symbolic of the oil burned for eight days in the story of Chanukah.

lulav (LOO-lav): Sprigs of palm, myrtle, and willow tied together to form one branch. It is used in ceremony, in conjunction with the *etrog*, during the holiday of Sukkot.

matzah (MAH-tsah): The unleavened bread eaten during Passover. It can come in the form of a cracker, a ball, and even a breakfast cereal. Caution: eating a lot of matzah may give one lead-belly.

matzah brei (MAH-tsa BRYE): Yiddish for a popular dish traditionally served for breakfast during Passover. It is made by dipping matzah crackers in water and eggs, then frying them. It can be served with cottage cheese, syrup, powdered sugar, or other toppings.

mazal tov (MAH-zal TOV): Hebrew for "good luck." It is a congratulatory expression said at weddings, bar and bat mitzvah celebrations, births, or other milestones.

megillah (meh-GIL-ah): Hebrew for "scroll." Used in Yiddish to mean "the whole ball of wax." One of the most well-known of the biblical scrolls is the Book of Esther, read on the holiday of Purim. This particular story is chanted out loud on Purim, giving birth to the expression, "the whole megillah."

menorah (meh-NOE-rah): A candelabra that holds seven candles. The nine-candled version, associated with Chanukah, is technically called a *Chanukiyah*. It has eight candles to represent the eight nights of the holiday, plus a "helper" candle, called the *shamash*, used to light the others. Today, menorahs come in all shapes and sizes, including ones that have Mickey Mouse and other Disney characters as candleholders.

mensch (MENCH): Yiddish for a nice, decent, honorable person.

milchig (MILL-khick): In kosher terms, the dairy foods (e.g., milk, cheese). When keeping kosher, it is prohibited to include meat products in a *milchig* meal.

mishpachah (mish-PUH-khah): This is the Yiddish pronunciation of the Hebrew word of the same spelling. It literally means "family." The "whole *mishpachah*" refers to everyone in the family, including extended family, relatives, and sometimes close friends.

mohel (MOY-el): A Hebrew word (MOE-hel), but often pronounced in this Yiddish version. It refers to the trained professional who performs the ritual circumcision at a bris.

Motzi (MOE-tsee): Short for *HaMotzi*, the blessing over the bread. Almost always, the bread is challah.

punim (PUH-nim): Yiddish for "face." Often said as part of the expression *shayna punim*, or "pretty face." Children duck for cover when hearing this phrase for fear of pinched cheeks.

seder (SAY-der): The ceremonial dinner of Passover, during which Jews read from the Haggadah, learn about the holiday, and eat great food.

Shabbat (shah-BAHT): The Jewish Sabbath. It begins on Friday at sundown and ends Saturday at sundown. It is traditionally a time when no work should be done.

Shabbes (SHA-bis): Yiddish for "Shabbat," the Jewish Sabbath.

Shabbes goy (SHA-bis GOY): The Yiddish term for a non-Jew who has been hired (often by a synagogue) to perform various jobs that are forbidden on Shabbat.

shiksa (SHICK-sah): A derogatory Yiddish term for a non-Jewish woman or girl.

shivah (SHIH-vah): The seven-day period of mourning immediately following burial. During this time, the grieving family members primarily stay in the home and receive those paying a condolence call. It is also called "sitting shivah."

sh'loshim (sheh-loe-SHEEM): The thirty-day period of mourning. The first seven days are called shivah. Between shivah and the end of the thirty days, the mourner is expected to resume normal activities, except for celebrations, sporting events, and other entertainment.

shmuck (SHMUCK): Despite many gentiles' cavalier use of this word, it is actually a vulgar Yiddish term for "penis."

shmutz (SHMUTZ): A Yiddish word for dirt, grime, or filth.

shofar (SHOW-far): A trumpet made from a ram's horn. It is blown at services on the holidays of Rosh HaShanah and Yom Kippur.

shtick (SHTICK): This Yiddish term is most commonly used for an actor's comedic routine. However, it can simply refer to anyone's clichéd mannerisms.

shul (SHOOL): Yiddish word for synagogue. Sometimes spelled schul.

shvitz (SHVITS): In Yiddish, when used as a verb, it means "to sweat;" as a noun, it means "steam bath." In Hebrew, it means to "boast or brag."

simchah (SIM-khah): A happy occasion. This is the Yiddish pronunciation. (In Hebrew, sim-KHA.)

sukkah (SOO-kah); pl., **sukkot** (soo-COTE): The hut built for the fall festival of Sukkot. During this time, families often eat and even sleep in the sukkah. It is symbolic of the temporary huts that the Jews carried with them as they wandered the desert with Moses. Caution to non-Jews who have not mastered the Jewish "u" sound. This "u" is pronounced as the "u" in "put" or the "oo" sound in "foot"—not as the "u" in "sucka."

Sukkot (soo-COTE): The fall harvest festival that commemorates the Exodus out of Egypt by Moses and the Israelites and gratitude for the blessings of the earth.

synagogue (SIN-a-gog): The English word for the Jewish place of worship. It is also known as "temple" or the Yiddish *shul* (SHOOL).

temple: Another English word for the Jewish place of worship.

Torah (TOE-rah): The first five books of the Bible: Genesis, Exodus, Leviticus, Numbers, and Deuteronomy. Many use this word as an abbreviation for *sefer Torah*. This refers to the scroll in a synagogue, which contains this history of the Jewish people.

Tribe, member of the: An expression for "member of the Jewish people." It originates from the twelve tribes of Israel, descended from Jacob's twelve sons.

verklempt (ver-KLEMPT): Most famously used by Mike Myers of "Saturday Night Live" fame, this word has worked its way into the vocabulary of Jews and non-Jews alike. It basically means "choked up" or "about to cry." Myers, who was at the time in an interfaith marriage, would use this term while imitating his Jewish mother-in-law on the TV show. "I'm getting a little *verklempt*. Talk amongst yourselves."

yahrzeit (YAHR-tsite): A Yiddish term referring to the anniversary of a loved one's death.

yarmulke (YAH-mi-kah): The Yiddish word for the skullcap worn as a sign of reverence. Some Jews wear them just in temple and at Jewish ceremonies. Some wear them everywhere. Some do not wear them at all. In Hebrew, it is called a *kippah* (KEE-pah). They are traditionally worn only by men, but today non-Orthodox women wear them as well.

Bibliography

Case, Edmund, ed. *The Guide to Jewish Interfaith Family Life: An Interfaithfamily .com Handbook*. Woodstock, VT: Jewish Lights Publishing, 2001.

Diamant, Anita. *The New Jewish Baby Book: Names, Ceremonies and Customs: A Guide for Today's Families*. Woodstock, VT: Jewish Lights Publishing, 1993.

Eisenberg, Joyce, and Ellen Scolnic. *The JPS Dictionary of Jewish Words*. Philadelphia: Jewish Publication Society, 2001.

Forman, Sharon. *Honest Answers to Your Child's Jewish Questions*. New York: URJ Press, 2006.

Judson, Dan, and Nancy H. Wiener. *Meeting at the Well: A Jewish Spiritual Guide to Being Engaged*. New York: UAHC Press, 2001.

Levin, Sunie. *Mingled Roots: A Guide for Grandparents of Interfaith Grandchildren*. New York: UAHC Press, 2003.

Syme, Daniel B. *The Jewish Home: A Guide for Jewish Living,* rev. ed. New York: URJ Press, 2004.

A discussion guide for this book can be found at
http://www.urjbooksandmusic.com

For more information and resources about interfaith marriage, please visit the
Web site for the URJ Department of Outreach and Synagogue Community at
http://ww.urj.org/outreach/.